IRS Tax Secrets

IRS Tax Secrets

The Individual and Small Business Owner's Guide to Solving IRS and State Tax Problems

JK Harris

Ep Entrepreneur® Press

Publisher: Jere Calmes
Cover Design: AndrewWelyczko, CWL Publishing Enterprises, Inc.
Editorial and Production Services: CWL Publishing Enterprises, Inc., Madison, Wisconsin, www.cwlpub.com

Copyright © 2011 by JK Harris. All rights reserved.

Reproduction of any part of this work beyond that permitted by Section 107 or 108 of the 1976 United States Copyright Act without the express permission of the copyright owner is unlawful. Requests for permission or further information should be addressed to the Business Products Division, Entrepreneur Media, Inc.

This publication is designed to provide accurate and authoritative information in regard to the subject matter covered. It is sold with the understanding that the publisher is not engaged in rendering legal, accounting, or other professional services. If legal advice or other expert assistance is required, the services of a competent professional person should be sought.
—From a Declaration of Principles jointly adopted by a Committee of the American Bar Association and a Committee of Publishers and Associations

ISBN 13: 978-1-59918-417-3
10: 1-59918-417-6

Every effort has been made to ensure that the information in this book is accurate and current at the time of publication. However, laws, regulations, policies, contact information, and so on may be changed without notice. This book is not a substitute for individual advice rendered by a professional who is able to work with you one-on-one.

Contents

1. Getting Started: Understanding the IRS and the Personal Impact of Tax Debt   1
What Tax Debt Means to You Personally   2
IRS Policy P-5-100 Offer in Compromise   4
The Evolution of Negotiating Tax Debts   5
A Brief History of the IRS   6
IRS Restructuring and Reform Act of 1998   7
Highlights   9

2. How Did You Get to This Point?   11
Can the IRS Send You to Jail?   13
Don't Sign or File a Return Unless You Understand It   14
Are You an Innocent Spouse?   17
Income from Criminal Activities Is Still Income   17
    Are You an Injured Spouse?   18
Highlights   18

3. Settle Back Tax Debt   21
Can You Do It Yourself?   22
First Things First: How Much Do You Owe?   25
Understanding the IRS Collection Process   26
Your Rights as a Taxpayer   27
Practical Advice for Working with the IRS   27
    Be Courteous and Adopt a Collaborative Attitude   27

Timeliness and Responsiveness Are Critical	28
Keep Track of Your Contacts	28
Be Clear, Concise, and Neat	28
Provide a Clear, Accurate, and Honest Picture of Your Finances	30
Don't Work on Your Tax Problems When You Are Tired or Distracted	30
Stay of Collections	**31**
Utilize IRS Resources	31
What Are Your Options?	31
Guidelines for Borrowing from a Relative	**32**
Full Pay	32
Installment Agreement	32
Offer in Compromise	33
Currently Not Collectible	33
IRS Collection Notices	34
When You Paid but the IRS Says You Didn't	37
Statute of Limitations	39
Highlights	40
4. What You Need to Know About Interest and Penalties	**42**
You May Have to Pay Civil Penalties For …	**45**
Reducing or Abating Penalties	46
Highlights	48
5. Understanding Liens and Levies	**51**
The Federal Tax Lien Process	52
Getting a Federal Tax Lien Released	53
Self-Releasing Liens	53
Withdrawal of Notice of Federal Tax Lien	54
Social Security Number (SSN) Redaction for Notice of Federal Tax Lien	**55**
IRS Tax Levies	55
Highlights	57

Contents

6. Offer in Compromise: Can You Really Settle for Less Than You Owe?   59
  Offer in Compromise—Doubt as to Collectibility   61
  Offer in Compromise—Doubt as to Liability   61
  Offer in Compromise—Effective Tax Administration   62
  Moving Forward with the Offer Process   63
  Basic Qualification for Offer in Compromise   63
  Offer in Compromise—General Conditions and Criteria Checklist   64
  OIC—Doubt as to Collectibility: Are You Eligible?   64
    Is This an Option for You?   65
    Offer in Compromise Worksheet 1   67
    Offer in Compromise Worksheet 2   68
    Offer in Compromise Worksheet 3   69
    Offer in Compromise Worksheet 4   69
    Worksheet Analysis   70
  Compiling Your Financial Information   71
  Checklist for Gathering Your Financial Records   72
  Preparing and Submitting Your Offer   74
    How Much Should You Offer?   74
    Preparing Your Package   74
  What's Next?   76
  Highlights   77

7. Installment Agreements: Paying Back Taxes Over Time   79
  Guaranteed Agreement   81
  Streamlined Agreement   81
  High Dollar Agreement   81
  Partial Payment Agreement   82
  Setting Up an Installment Agreement   83
  Highlights   83

8. Communicating with the IRS   85
  How to Use the IRS Letter Worksheet to Write Your Letter   87
  Highlights   88
  IRS Letter Worksheet   89

Sample Letters	90
Sample Letter: Offer in Compromise—	
Effective Tax Administration	*91*
Sample Letter: Offer in Compromise—	
Effective Tax Administration	*92*
Sample Letter: Offer in Compromise—	
Doubt as to Liability	*93*
Sample Letter: Requesting an Abatement of Penalties	*94*
IRS Communication Record	95

9. When You Fail to Pay Your Payroll Taxes — 97
The Trust Fund Recovery Penalty — 98
Don't Wait to Take Action — 99
Highlights — 100

10. IRS Audits: Take Them Seriously, but Don't Panic — 101
Do You Need Representation? — **103**
Type of Audit—Matching — 103
Type of Audit—Correspondence — 104
Type of Audit—Office — 105
    Type of Audit—Field — 106
Type of Audit—Research — 108
Type of Audit—Criminal Investigation — 109
Seven Important Facts about Your Appeal Rights — **110**
How Does the IRS Select Returns for Examination? — 111
How Are You Notified That You Are Being Audited? — 112
Highlights — 113

11. Other Taxing Authorities — 115
Criminal Liability for Back State Taxes — 117
Knowledge Is Your Best Defense — 118
Where to Go for State Tax Information — 118
Highlights — 118

12. Go It Alone or Get Help? — 121
Should You Do It Yourself? — 122
    Doing It Yourself — *122*
Hiring Someone to Help and Represent You — 123

Who Can Represent You Before the IRS?	124
Selecting the Right Representation	125
Using an Online Tax Representation Service	125
Tips for Choosing a Tax Representation Firm	125
Highlights	127
13. Stay in Compliance	**129**
Be Proactive	129
Keep Good Records	130
We're Here to Help	131
Terms You Need to Know	**133**
Acronyms and Abbreviations	151
Resources for State Tax Information	**153**
About JK Harris	**209**

Preface

If you are reading this book, it is likely you owe money to the IRS. An estimated 12 million U.S. households report that they currently owe or have owed back taxes, so you are not alone. You are in a situation that could range from moderately difficult to extremely challenging, depending on how much you owe and your circumstances—but there is a solution and we are going to help you find it.

Our market research indicates that only about 2 million of the 12 million households that are in debt to the IRS will seek professional assistance in dealing with their problem. The vast majority of taxpayers who owe back taxes either can't afford or, for a variety of reasons, simply aren't willing to pay a professional firm to represent them with the IRS. If you fall into that category, this book is for you. If you owe back taxes, this book will tell you what your options are and what steps you need to take to resolve your tax problem.

Since 1997, my firm has helped more than 250,000 clients deal with tax debt. With rare exceptions, our clients are not deliberate tax cheats. They are honest people who want to honor their obligations and pay their taxes, but something has happened in their lives that has made it difficult or impossible for them to do that. If that's the situation you're in, this book will help you figure out what to do and how to do it.

I want to stress that this book will not tell you how to avoid paying taxes, nor will it give you tax planning strategies. This is a book about what to do when you are in debt to the IRS or other taxing authorities and you can't afford to pay what you owe them.

My goal is to give you the knowledge and tools you need to end your tax nightmares forever. Yes, the first step is to deal with your immediate issues, whether you've received an audit notice, are facing liens or levies, or haven't filed tax returns in years. But once you are in compliance, you need a plan to stay that way, and I'm going to tell you how to do that, as well. I truly want you to be able to read this book, handle your situation, and implement a plan to stay out of tax debt forever.

Let's get started.

1

Getting Started: Understanding the IRS and the Personal Impact of Tax Debt

When you say "taxes," most U.S. taxpayers think first of the Internal Revenue Service (IRS), which is the federal tax collection agency that administers the Internal Revenue Code enacted by Congress. The IRS is arguably the most intimidating and feared of all government agencies. In spite of its many efforts to reform itself and rehabilitate its reputation, it remains a daunting, nerveracking behemoth that most taxpayers would rather avoid than face—and when you hear some of the nightmare stories told by taxpayers, it's easy to understand why.

Tales of strong-arm tactics and assessments of exorbitant penalties are not only legendary, they are a primary reason why the IRS is so successful at collecting monies owed—and sometimes even monies not owed. A taxpayer's willingness to be intimidated exacerbates a tax problem. Because they are intimidated, they often want to avoid any contact with the IRS, but refusing to deal with whatever is going on will only make a bad situation worse. As I'll explain, the

IRS is structured to encourage you to face your tax issues and get them handled, not to put them off. But that doesn't mean you should just obediently pay whatever the IRS says you should. Many taxpayers, even when they believe the IRS' position is not valid, will write a check because they don't think they can dispute it. But that isn't true, and I'm going to tell you how to handle that.

In addition to the IRS, there are a multitude of state and local taxing authorities you may have to deal with for various reasons—for example, if you are subject to state income tax; if you pay property taxes; if you have a business and pay various business taxes; and so on. We discuss those other taxing authorities in Chapter 11. However, in this book, we focus primarily on the IRS because that's the largest tax agency in the United States and many of the basic tactics and strategies you will use with the IRS can also be applied to those other agencies.

> **TAX FACT**
>
> The United States still functions under the Internal Revenue Code that was drafted by Congress in 1954 and has been amended virtually every year since. It began as a 300-page document and today includes more than 1 million pages. Accompanying the law are a staggering 2.5 million pages of regulations.

What Tax Debt Means to You Personally

Whether you own a company or are an individual taxpayer, owing back taxes can be devastating. The IRS can seize your cash and other assets through liens and levies. IRS actions can damage and even destroy your credit rating. Stress related to your situation can take its toll on your health and your relationships with your spouse, your other family members, your friends, and your business associates.

It can be overwhelming even if you don't actually owe the taxes but the IRS erroneously claims you do. That's what happened to Alex and Kay Council, who owned a homebuilding company in Winston-Salem, North Carolina, when the IRS notified them in 1983

Getting Started 3

that they owed $183,021 in taxes, penalties, and interest from their 1979 return—a figure that steadily increased over the years as the Councils attempted to deal with the bureaucratic jungle that was the IRS at the time. The case went to court in October 1988; after a non-jury trial, the judge found against the IRS and ordered the agency to drop its collection efforts and cancel the tax lien for $284,718 it had filed in 1987 against all of the Councils' assets. It was a victory Alex Council didn't see. In June 1988, crushed by the battle and seeing no other way, Alex killed himself to make funds available to Kay from his suicide-proof life insurance policy. In his suicide note, he wrote, "The IRS and its liens which have been taken against our property illegally by a runaway agency of our government have dried up all sources of credit for us. So I have made the only decision I can."

Much has changed at the IRS since that tragedy, including the creation of the Taxpayer Bill of Rights and the Taxpayer Advocate Service, and the general structure of the agency through the IRS Restructuring and Reform Act of 1998. Today's IRS consists of two primary divisions: one that assesses taxes and one that collects them. The assessment division is part of the IRS that receives your tax returns and will also prepare them for you if you request it or if you fail to file your returns yourself, and then assesses what you owe.

At this point, if you do not agree with the assessment, you have the right to a due process collection hearing to argue your case before enforced collections begin. If the IRS doesn't accept your position or if you do not respond to the assessment notice, and you do not pay the tax due, the file moves over to the collections side. Most taxpayers deal with the assessment side of the IRS once a year by filing their tax returns and they rarely have any other interactions with the IRS. My firm deals primarily with the collections side, because that's the point at which our clients need help.

TAX FACT

In the early 1950s, the IRS stopped automatically preparing tax returns for all American taxpayers. This policy change allowed Henry and Richard Bloch to create H&R Block—now the world's largest tax preparation firm.

What's important to recognize is that even though the IRS has worked hard to improve and continues to do so, mistakes are still made, both on the part of the IRS as well as the taxpayer, and the process of dealing with the agency remains painfully slow.

This is why, whether you actually owe the money or not, it's critical that you address your back tax situation as quickly and efficiently as possible. Completing the actual resolution can be a lengthy process, but simply getting it underway will help reduce your stress level and help you get your life back under control.

IRS POLICY P-5-100 OFFER IN COMPROMISE

1. Offers will be accepted: The Service will accept an offer in compromise when it is unlikely that the tax liability can be collected in full and the amount offered reasonably reflects collection potential. An offer in compromise is a legitimate alternative to declaring a case currently not collectible or to a protracted installment agreement. The goal is to achieve collection of what is potentially collectible at the earliest possible time and at the least cost to the Government.

2. In cases where an offer in compromise appears to be a viable solution to a tax delinquency, the Service employee assigned the case will discuss the compromise alternative with the taxpayer and, when necessary, assist in preparing the required forms. The taxpayer will be responsible for initiating the first specific proposal for compromise.

3. The success of the compromise program will be assured only if taxpayers make adequate compromise proposals consistent with their ability to pay and the Service makes prompt and reasonable decisions. Taxpayers are expected to provide reasonable documentation to verify their ability to pay. The ultimate goal is a compromise that is in the best interest of both the taxpayer and the Service. Acceptance of an adequate offer will also result in creating for the taxpayer an expectation of and a fresh start toward compliance with all future filing and payment requirements.

The Evolution of Negotiating Tax Debts

Prior to January 1992, the IRS in general did not compromise tax debt, meaning that it would not negotiate on the amount due. Individuals who owed taxes were simply at the mercy of the IRS. If the tax debt was valid, you had to pay it—one way or another. Though there were exceptions, they were few and rare, and they were made for very complicated cases. There were no rules or guidelines for the process; the compromise was negotiated on an individual basis.

People who owed back taxes were put on what amounted to a lifetime installment agreement. On paper, the agreement was for 10 years, but in many cases, the monthly payment was not enough to cover the interest and penalties. You could pay for 10 years and owe more than you did at the start. At that point, the IRS would roll the agreement forward for another 10 years and you would keep getting deeper and deeper in debt. The problem for the IRS was that when people figured out they could never get their tax debt paid, they would stop trying. In some years, the default rate on the installment agreements was above 85 percent. Back then, it was much easier than it is today for people to essentially go underground and work for cash. They would move, not leave a forwarding address, and it would take the IRS years to find them.

So in January 1992, IRS Policy Statement P-5-100 was issued, offering people who owed back taxes a chance to settle their debt and move on with their lives. It also created the tax representation industry, because even though the language of the policy statement sounds simple enough, the actual process of negotiating an offer in compromise can be complex and time-consuming.

> **RESPECTFULLY QUOTED**
> "In 1790, the nation which had fought a revolution against taxation without representation discovered that some of its citizens weren't much happier about taxation with representation."
> —*Lyndon B. Johnson*

I didn't know much about this when I opened my accounting practice in Charleston in 1997. I had a comfortable client base of small businesses that I worked with, and I was enjoying helping

A BRIEF HISTORY OF THE IRS

The roots of the IRS go back to the Civil War when President Lincoln and Congress, in 1862, created the position of commissioner of Internal Revenue and enacted an income tax to pay war expenses. The income tax was repealed 10 years later. Congress revived the income tax in 1894, but the Supreme Court ruled it unconstitutional the following year.

In 1913, Wyoming ratified the 16th Amendment, providing the three-quarter majority of states necessary to amend the Constitution. The 16th Amendment gave Congress the authority to enact an income tax. That same year, the first Form 1040 appeared after Congress levied a 1 percent tax on net personal incomes above $3,000 with a 6 percent surtax on incomes of more than $500,000.

In 1918, during World War I, the top rate of the income tax rose to 77 percent to help finance the war effort. It dropped sharply in the post-war years, down to 24 percent in 1929, and rose again during the Depression. During World War II, Congress introduced payroll withholding and quarterly tax payments.

In the 1950s, the agency was reorganized to replace a patronage system with career, professional employees. The Bureau of Internal Revenue name was changed to the Internal Revenue Service. Only the IRS commissioner and chief counsel are selected by the President and confirmed by the Senate.

---

them with their business and financial strategies. I had signed a new client, a small retail shop in downtown Charleston that was owned by a British woman who was married to an American oil industry executive. A few weeks later, I got a call from the husband. They were selling their house and the title search showed several large federal tax liens against him attached to the property. He asked me if I could figure out what that was all about. So I headed off to the courthouse and confirmed the liens; then I went to the store to talk to his wife. When I asked my client if she'd received any correspondence from the IRS, she quite cheerfully admitted that she had. When I asked what she had done with it, she pulled open a drawer

IRS RESTRUCTURING AND REFORM ACT OF 1998

The IRS Restructuring and Reform Act of 1998 prompted the most comprehensive reorganization and modernization of the IRS in nearly half a century. The IRS reorganized itself to resemble the private sector model of organizing around customers with similar needs. To support its structure and ensure accountability, the IRS is divided into three commissioner-level organizations:

Commissioner. Specialized IRS units report directly to the Commissioner's office. The IRS Chief Counsel also reports to the Treasury General Counsel on certain matters.

Deputy Commissioner for Services and Enforcement. The Deputy Commissioner reports directly to the Commissioner and oversees the four primary operating divisions (Wage and Investment Division, Large Business and International Division, Small Business/Self-Employed Division, and Tax Exempt and Government Entities Division) and other service and enforcement functions (Criminal Investigation, Office of Professional Responsibility, and Whistleblower Office).

Deputy Commissioner for Operations Support. The Deputy Commissioner reports directly to the Commissioner and oversees the integrated IRS support functions, facilitating economy of scale efficiencies and better business practices.

More important is that this Act provides for taxpayer protection and rights, shifting the burden of proof with respect to a factual issue in any court proceeding from the taxpayer to the Internal Revenue Service; broadens the scope and amount of administrative costs and attorney's fees that may be awarded to a taxpayer who substantially prevails in any action by or against the United States in connection with the determination, collection or refund of tax, interest or penalties; increases the scope of civil damages that may be awarded to taxpayers as a result of an officer or employee of the IRS recklessly or intentionally disregarding the provisions of the IRS Code or regulations to include damages resulting from negligent acts by IRS personnel; and other protections and services for taxpayers.

and showed me a huge stack of certified mail from the IRS that she had not even opened.

It seems that because she was a British subject, she wasn't sure if she could legally own a business in the United States (she could, but that's another issue), so she put everything related to her company in her husband's name. She knew nothing about the American tax system and didn't bother to learn. She had employees and for years had not withheld or paid payroll taxes on their earnings. She wasn't bothering to collect and remit sales tax to the state. And when the IRS began hounding her, she decided the best way to deal with the situation was to ignore it. Unfortunately for her and her husband, the IRS doesn't ignore people who owe back taxes, so it went after the assets of her husband because that's whose name was on all the business documents.

I called her husband and explained the situation, and he asked me if I could handle settling the back tax debt of $90,000 with the IRS and get the liens removed. That was my practical introduction to the offer in compromise program. I found a former IRS agent who knew the ropes, and we were successful in negotiating settlement of $42,000—less than half of what was owed.

In the process, I realized that there were millions of people who owed money to the IRS that they couldn't pay and there was a tremendous need in the marketplace for a firm that could help them. So I launched JK Harris & Company and within a few years we were the nation's largest tax representation firm.

Since then, a number of other companies have jumped into the business, creating some strong and healthy competition that has been good for us and good for consumers. If you owe a tax debt you can't afford to pay, you have plenty of options when it comes to getting help in dealing with it—and if you want to handle it yourself, you can do it that way as well. This book will show you how.

Getting Started

HIGHLIGHTS

- The Internal Revenue Service (IRS) is the federal tax collection agency that administers the Internal Revenue Code enacted by Congress.
- In addition to the IRS, there are a multitude of state and local taxing authorities you may have to deal with for various reasons.
- Owing back taxes can be devastating in a variety of ways. The IRS can seize your cash and other assets through liens and levies; damage your credit rating; and inflict stress that can affect your health and relationships.
- If the IRS notifies you that you owe back taxes, it is critical that you address the situation immediately, whether or not you actually owe the money.
- Prior to 1992, the IRS rarely negotiated the amount due on tax debt.
- In 1992, IRS Policy P-5-100 established the policy under which the IRS will accept an offer in compromise, which is a program where taxpayers who are unable to pay the full amount due can offer a reduced amount in settlement of their tax debt.
- The IRS Restructuring and Reform Act of 1998 reorganized the IRS and provided for the Taxpayer Bill of Rights and the Taxpayer Advocate Service.

2

How Did You Get to This Point?

Certainly one of life's greatest headaches is associated with paying taxes. Keeping records, using the right forms, understanding the instructions, doing the math, and writing that final check is generally not a happily anticipated life event. And if just preparing your annual federal and state tax returns causes your temples to pound, then an unexpected letter of inquiry from the IRS or an audit notice will create a headache of migraine proportions. Keeping straight on your taxes is not easy when you have the money to pay what you owe—and when you can't afford to pay, your problems are multiplied exponentially.

Having back tax debt is nothing to be ashamed of. It happens to a lot of people—decent, honest people who want to pay their obligations, people who call our offices every day looking for help. The stories you hear about in the news about people who are essentially tax cheats are the minority.

There are a variety of ways honest people get into tax debt. In many cases, it starts with a relatively low tax bill and snowballs.

Let's say for some reason your employer didn't withhold enough out of your paychecks to cover your full tax liability. At the end of the year, you're going to owe the IRS money. If you can't afford to pay that, the amount is going to quickly build due to interest and penalties (which we talk more about in later chapters).

People who are self-employed are responsible for making quarterly tax payments to the IRS. That takes a lot of self-discipline, especially if you're dealing with other financial issues. And again, it can snowball. You skip the first payment, then the second, then the third, and before you know it, it's time to file your return and you've made no quarterly payments and you're facing a huge tax bill. Along these lines, it's common for small business owners who have employees to miss submitting their payroll tax reports and payments—something the IRS doesn't tolerate at all.

Something else we're starting to see among our clients is that a lot of people had to tap into their retirement accounts during the recent recession. Many of them took that money out without fully considering the tax implications and didn't set enough aside to pay the taxes on the withdrawal. A couple of years later, the IRS is going to catch up with them and hit them with a tax bill they may not be able to pay.

Many times people who are in debt to the IRS are simply procrastinators. They put off filing their returns, they put off responding to IRS correspondence, they put off paying their tax bills. Some of them procrastinate because they're busy with work and family; some procrastinate because they have emotional and/or mental health issues that make it difficult if not impossible for them to just sit down and prepare their tax returns. In fact, about 50 percent of JK Harris' new clients have not filed a tax return in at least four years.

If you are earning money that is being reported to the IRS and you do not file tax returns, the IRS will eventually do it for you. But those returns will not be filed to your advantage; they will not include any deductions or allowances, or anything else that might reduce your tax obligation. That happens because the people who are paying you have to report those payments to the government. Eventually that information gets to the IRS, who checks to see if the payment shows up on a corresponding tax return—something we discuss in Chapter 10 when we talk about audits. When the IRS can't match a payment reported by one taxpayer to income on a tax return filed by the person who received the payment, troubles have begun.

> **TAX FACT**
>
> There is no back tax amount that is too small for the IRS to pursue. Small amounts may be processed differently and require different documentation when seeking a settlement than large amounts, but in general, the IRS does not differentiate between liability amounts. If you owe any amount of back taxes, you need to take care of the situation.

Can the IRS Send You to Jail?

Many people are afraid of the IRS because they hear stories about people going to jail for owing taxes. Those stories represent a very small fraction of the people who owe back taxes and usually involve fraud that goes beyond simply not paying your federal taxes. The IRS itself does not send people to jail; it can recommend that a case be prosecuted, and if that happens, federal prosecutors will get involved.

When people who have not paid their taxes go to jail, it is because there was a crime associated with the situation. When you try to avoid paying taxes by committing a fraud such as failing to report income or knowingly lying on your tax return, you risk being charged with tax evasion or fraud and prosecuted by the U.S. Attorney's office.

You've probably heard stories of famous people who went to prison at least in part because of tax fraud. The best the government could do against notorious gangster Al Capone was to convict him of tax evasion for not reporting the income he earned on his criminal activities. In 1931, he was fined and sentenced to 11 years in prison.

> **DON'T SIGN OR FILE A RETURN UNLESS YOU UNDERSTAND IT**
>
> It's important to keep in mind that not all tax preparers are created equal. Their degree of knowledge, professional skill, and even ethics can vary tremendously. It is not unusual for a back tax liability to be caused by an error by the preparer. Even if the preparer is at fault, you are responsible for the tax that would have been due had your return been done correctly and you may still be assessed interest and penalties.
>
> We have seen extreme cases where preparers take tax credits the client isn't entitled to, list bogus expenses, and even claim more dependents than the taxpayer actually has. Those taxpayers tell us quite candidly that they didn't look at the return; they just signed it. But when you sign a tax return, you are declaring under penalties of perjury that you have examined the return and that it is true, correct, and complete to the best of your knowledge. Take the time to review your return and be sure it is indeed true, correct, and complete.

Decades later, hotelier Leona Helmsley, known as the Queen of Mean, spent four years in prison for tax fraud after claiming some $2.6 million in phony business expenses. Rock and roll legend Chuck Berry spent four months in prison for getting paid in cash and not reporting that income. And Hollywood Madame Heidi Fleiss went to prison for pandering, money laundering, and tax evasion.

Does the government like to make examples of famous people in the hope of deterring ordinary folks from committing tax fraud? I don't know. But I believe if the government feels it has a valid case against someone, it will prosecute regardless of their celebrity or non-celebrity status.

Here's a sampling of some of the cases where "ordinary" people were prosecuted for tax-related crimes:

- In 2008, seven people in Georgia were sentenced to prison and/or home confinement for participating in a scheme involving filing fraudulent claims for tax refunds based on fictitious diesel fuel tax credits. When businesses purchase diesel fuel on which federal excise taxes have already been paid (known as "undyed fuel") and use that fuel in off-highway business equipment, the businesses qualify for a tax credit for the excise taxes paid. However, the claims for refund in this investigation were fraudulent because the defendants did not purchase, nor did they use, the undyed fuel in their off-highway business equipment. The seven defendants sentenced were collectively responsible for fraudulent claims for federal income tax refunds totaling $3,214,231. This wasn't an innocent tax mistake.

- In another case, Joseph William Hughes of Minneapolis, a registered representative of a legitimate financial service company, concocted a scheme to embezzle money from an elderly couple's accounts. He was caught and he pled guilty to one count of mail fraud and one count of tax evasion. He was sentenced to 46 months in prison and ordered to pay $456,970 in restitution. The mail fraud charge arose because he used the mail when he was embezzling the funds; the tax evasion charge came because he did not report the money he stole from his clients as income. The funds embezzled by Hughes were income that he was required to report on his income tax returns. However, Hughes willfully attempted to evade and defeat a large part of the income tax due by preparing false and fraudulent income tax returns. Yes, there is more than a little irony in the fact that the law says you must report all your income—even illegal income—or you can be charged with tax evasion. Hughes could have learned a lesson from Al Capone.

- In 2009, a Texas doctor, Malcolm David MacHauer, was sentenced to 33 months imprisonment, to be followed by three years of supervised release, and ordered to pay restitution in the amount of $222,782. A jury found him guilty of three counts of attempting to evade and defeat paying federal income taxes. According to information presented in court, although MacHauer received income from Wadley Medical Center in Texarkana, Texas, for his services as a doctor, he failed to pay the appropriate federal income taxes. Instead, MacHauer placed his income into his corporation, transferred the money to the

MacHauer Family Trust, and then withdrew money from that trust to pay his personal expenses without paying income tax. If you're trying to pull a stunt like this one, you can stop reading right now because this book will not help you.

- Another group of people who are likely to be the target of aggressive criminal prosecution are the tax protestors, who generally believe that the income tax laws are invalid or do not apply to most citizens and therefore they have a legal and moral right to not pay their taxes. Tax protestors engage in a variety of schemes from simply refusing to pay taxes to large-scale scams and frauds, and have been known to resort to violence including attacking IRS agents and property or other law enforcement agents. If anyone tells you that filing tax returns violates your Fifth Amendment rights, that the Sixteenth Amendment was never properly ratified, that wages are not income, or that income taxes are voluntary, don't listen. If those people follow their own advice, they are likely to end up in jail—and if you follow their advice, you could join them.

My point in relaying these stories is this: If you are simply unable to pay your taxes because you do not have the money but you are not attempting to defraud the government and you're working on a resolution, you do not need to worry about the government filing criminal charges. As Oliver Wendell Holmes wrote, "Even a dog distinguishes between being stumbled over and being kicked."

> **RESPECTFULLY QUOTED**
>
> "The best measure of a man's honesty isn't his income tax return. It's the zero adjust on his bathroom scale."
>
> —Arthur C. Clarke

Are You an Innocent Spouse?

Not every marriage ends in happily ever after, and the IRS recognizes that. If your spouse or former spouse improperly reported

How Did You Get to This Point?

items or omitted items on your tax return, you can be relieved of responsibility for paying tax, interest, and penalties on those items if you qualify for innocent spouse relief.

To qualify for innocent spouse relief, you must meet all of the following conditions:

- You filed a joint return that has an understatement of tax due to erroneous items (unreported income; incorrect deduction, credit or basis) of your spouse or former spouse.

- You establish that at the time you signed the joint return you did not know, and had no reason to know, that there was an understatement of tax.

- Taking into account all the facts and circumstances, it would be unfair to hold you liable for the understatement of tax.

INCOME FROM CRIMINAL ACTIVITIES IS STILL INCOME

Federal regulations require you to report your income—all of it, regardless of how you earned it, even if you earned it by committing a crime. As crazy as it sounds, if you rob a bank and get away with it, you are supposed to report the money you stole as income on your tax return—and plenty of criminals do exactly that. Prostitutes, for example, may report their source of income as "private entertainment," which is not illegal. Drug dealers may report their source of income as "pharmaceutical sales." People who commit other types of criminal activity may list the income simply as "other" on their tax returns.

Please understand this: I am not condoning or in any way encouraging any type of criminal conduct. But it's important that you know that any money you make from criminal activity is still income and should be treated as such on your tax return. And if you are ever audited by the IRS (see Chapter 10 for more about the audit process), there's a good chance the examiner will compare your lifestyle to your reported income. If you appear to be living beyond your means—that is, if your lifestyle is one that couldn't be supported by the income you are reporting—it could spark a criminal investigation into both the underreporting of income as well as the possibility of criminal conduct to earn income.

Be aware that a request for innocent spouse relief will not be granted if the IRS proves that you and your spouse or former spouse transferred property to one another as part of a fraudulent scheme. A fraudulent scheme includes a scheme to defraud the IRS or another third party, such as a creditor, ex-spouse, or business partner.

To apply for innocent spouse relief, you must complete Form 8857 and attach a statement explaining why you qualify.

Are You an Injured Spouse?

Different than an innocent spouse, an injured spouse is someone who files a joint return where a refund is due, and then all or part of the injured spouse's share of the refund was kept by the IRS and applied toward the other spouse's past due debts. The injured spouse can get a refund for his or her share of the overpayment.

To be considered an injured spouse, you must have made and reported tax payments (federal income tax withheld from wages or estimated tax payments) or claimed a refundable tax credit such as the earned income credit or additional child tax credit on the joint return and not be legally obligated to pay the past due tax amount.

HIGHLIGHTS

- Owing back taxes is nothing to be ashamed of. There are a variety of ways honest people get into tax debt.
- Interest and penalties charged by the IRS can turn a manageable tax liability into an overwhelming debt.
- If you do not file your own tax returns and are earning money that is being reported to the IRS, the IRS will eventually file your returns for you. The IRS does not include deductions, allowances, or anything else that will reduce your tax liability when it does this.
- Never sign or file a return unless you know what it contains, understand everything that's on it, and know that every item being reported is accurate and true.

- The IRS does not send people to jail; instead, when it identifies criminal activity, it refers the case to federal prosecutors.
- Tax protestors are those people who believe they have a legal and moral right to not pay their taxes. These people often participate in illegal activities and the IRS pursues them aggressively.
- Innocent spouse relief may be requested when your spouse or former spouse improperly reported or omitted items on your tax return and the IRS determines that it would be unfair to hold you liable for the tax.
- Injured spouse relief may be available when a joint return is filed and any refund is applied to the back taxes of one spouse which the other spouse is not responsible for paying.
- If you earn income from criminal activities, you must report that income and pay taxes on it.

3

Settle Back Tax Debt

The first step in resolving your back tax problems is deciding to do it—and that sounds far simpler and easier than it really is. For most people, getting into tax debt is a lot like gaining weight. You gain weight a little at a time; the first few pounds are barely noticeable, then your clothes are getting snug, then tight, then you have to get a larger size. Over a period of time, you've gone from a healthy weight to slightly chubby to fat to obese—and when you hit obese, you're not only dealing with the way you look and the way your clothes fit, you've also likely got some serious health problems.

For most of us, tax debt happens much the same way. At first, it's likely a relatively small amount of money that you don't pay for some reason and nobody is bugging you about it. Then the amount you owe begins to increase and you start to get the occasional notice from the IRS. Next, the interest and penalties are assessed, and that relatively small amount of money has turned into a substantial amount. Time passes and your tax debt has grown from chubby to obese, and you've got some serious financial problems.

> **RESPECTFULLY QUOTED**
> "To tax and to please, no more than to love and to be wise, is not given to men."
> —Edmund Burke

If you owe back taxes, the most difficult thing you have to do is make the commitment to deal with the situation. The process won't be a walk in the park—but if you make the commitment, do your homework, put together a plan, and follow through, you can eventually end your tax nightmare.

Can You Do It Yourself?

Can you resolve your back tax issues yourself, dealing directly with the IRS without professional help? The short answer is yes, you can. Should you? That's a more complicated question, and it depends on how much you owe, your particular circumstances, and your own personal tolerance for dealing with a high degree of frustration as a result of the IRS bureaucracy. After you finish this book, you should have enough information to make that decision.

I'm sure you've seen and heard plenty of ads for companies that provide tax resolution services—they're all over television, radio, and the internet. You've probably also seen a significant number of ads for JK Harris & Company's professional tax representation services. There's an important difference between tax resolution and tax representation. Resolution is exactly what it says—it's the end of the process when the tax debt is resolved. And it's a very small portion of the tax representation process, which is the professional service involved in assisting delinquent taxpayers so that a resolution can be reached. Tax representation includes dealing with the IRS on your behalf, helping you get in compliance by preparing and filing your past due and currently due tax returns (including income, payroll, self-employment, and others), representing you during an audit, analyzing your situation to determine your resolution options, presenting your resolution to the IRS, representing you during any appeals you may choose to file, and so on.

Every tax resolution and representation firm wants your business—and we are no exception. However, even though we definitely want your business, I'm the first person to say that not everyone who owes back taxes needs a professional to help them get the situation resolved. For example, if you're just a year or two behind in filing or if the amount you owe is relatively small, you can probably handle your case yourself and save the fees a professional would charge. For example, it would be silly for you to pay a professional $2,000 or $3,000 to help you settle a tax debt of $3,000. That's why we offer an initial consultation at no cost—it's not unusual for us to tell a prospective client after our first meeting that he doesn't really need us. One of the reasons I wrote this book was to provide information for the people who have a problem but it's not to the point where it requires professional assistance.

This book will also help those people whose problem might be more complex but they just prefer to handle things themselves. If you're not sure which category you're in, I invite you to call us for a free, no-obligation consultation so that you can make an informed decision about the best way to handle your situation.

As an alternative, you can start with our online service by going to www.JKHarrisTaxHelpOnline.com where you can get an analysis of your situation with recommendations about the next steps you need to take. This service is designed to assist you while also allowing you to make your own decision about how much you want to do yourself, when you need a consultation with a professional, and if you want to turn your entire case over to a professional representative to deal with the IRS on your behalf.

While it is definitely possible for anyone to handle their own tax issues without professional representation, and while I do believe that many individuals can successfully do just that, I want to stress at this point that I do not recommend trying to negotiate with the IRS on your own if you are a business owner. We talk about this in Chapter 9, but if you own your company (either as a sole proprietor, partner, or stockholder) and are behind in your business taxes, I recommend that you seek professional assistance immediately—the survival of your business depends on it.

Individual taxpayers will find that today's IRS is far easier to work with than the IRS of a decade ago. The agency has improved its technological systems, created written objectives to become more "customer friendly" (if you want to think of taxpayers as being the customers), has created the Office of Taxpayer Advocate, and has demonstrated increased receptivity to offers in compromise.

There has never been a better time for a taxpayer to attempt to work with the IRS to resolve a tax problem. A key reason is that real estate values, both residential and commercial, are lower than they've been in years. If you have a mortgage on your property, that means your equity (the difference between what you owe and what the property is worth) has been seriously reduced and perhaps even totally eliminated. As depressing as this might be for other reasons, it's great news if you're negotiating with the IRS. As you will learn in Chapter 6, when you make an offer in compromise, the IRS considers all your assets when determining what you can afford to pay. If you have no or minimal equity in your real estate, you won't be expected to use that equity through either the sale of the property or borrowing against it to pay your tax debt.

Before you decide whether or not to move forward with handling your tax situation yourself, read through this entire book so you have a solid understanding of what needs to be done. Then you can decide whether to do it yourself or if your time and resources are better spent retaining a tax representation firm to work with the IRS on your behalf. If you decide to seek help, having read this book will make you an informed client who knows what to expect during the process.

First Things First: How Much Do You Owe?

You cannot resolve your tax problems until you know exactly what they are—and to do that, you must be in compliance with IRS regu-

Settle Back Tax Debt

lations. That means to get your tax returns filed, if you haven't done so—even if you can't afford to send any money with the returns. This will let you know exactly how much you owe so you can decide what your next step should be.

You may file your taxes electronically for the current year only. Late returns must be filed on paper. If you are late, we recommend that you file all your returns at the same time, but if you are filing for more than one year, put each return in a separate envelope and send it by certified mail, return receipt requested.

You can purchase the major tax preparation software packages for previous years on websites such as H&R Block (www.hrblock.com) and TurboTax (www.turbotax.com). This will allow you to prepare your returns electronically but you must still print out all the completed documents and mail them to the IRS. You can get all the forms for free on the IRS website, but you'll have to fill them out by hand. Unless your returns are extremely simple, the software is a worthwhile investment. Some of the tax preparation software packages will deeply discount their versions for previous years or even provide it for free when you purchase the current year.

When filing your returns, do not skip any years. Start with the oldest year you haven't filed, and file them in order or all at the same time. Here's why you should not file your returns out of sequence: Let's say it's 2011 and you have not filed a return since 2006. If you file your 2010 return without filing your 2007, 2008, and 2009 returns and you are due a refund, the IRS will see that those three returns are missing and they will hold your refund until those returns are filed. Of course, if you are eligible for a refund for one year and owe for the others, the IRS is going to apply the refund to whatever you owe, and there is no way to get around that.

Once you're in compliance and know exactly what your tax liability is,

RESPECTFULLY QUOTED

"The hardest thing in the world to understand is the income tax."
—Albert Einstein

you can work on a plan to take care of the situation. We'll discuss your options shortly.

Understanding the IRS Collection Process

Do you know where you are in the IRS collection process? To answer that question, you need to understand the entire process and how it moves from simple notices up to and including property seizures. Believe me when I tell you that wherever you are in the process, you don't want to move any further. Don't put off answering notices or returning calls. Don't miss any more deadlines. That will only make things more complicated. The IRS is not going to go away—and it's not going to forget about you.

Regardless of how your tax debt came about, this is the IRS collection process:

You owe taxes
↓
Interest and penalties accrue on the balance due, increasing your tax bill substantially
↓
The IRS sends a series of notices
↓
The IRS sends a certified letter
↓
Your case is transferred to Automated Collection System (ACS) and someone from ACS may call you
↓
The IRS may file a federal tax lien or issue a levy on your bank or employer
↓
Your case is transferred to a revenue officer who will attempt to collect in person if necessary
↓
The IRS Collection Division will use a variety of collection methods including property seizure and will pursue the case until resolution or until the IRS is satisfied that it has tapped every available asset and income source you have

---

> **YOUR RIGHTS AS A TAXPAYER**
>
> Regardless of your status in terms of owing back taxes, you have rights as a taxpayer that should be explained and protected throughout your contacts with the IRS. Those rights include:
> - The right to professional and courteous treatment by IRS employees.
> - The right to privacy and confidentiality about tax matters.
> - The right to know why the IRS is asking for information, how the IRS will use the information, and what will happen if the requested information is not provided.
> - The right to representation by yourself or an authorized representative.
> - The right to appeal disagreements, both within the IRS and before the courts.

Practical Advice for Working with the IRS

You don't need an accounting or law degree to work effectively with the IRS, but you do need to use common sense. It's also important to recognize that while U.S. law is based on the concept of innocent until proven guilty, your dealings with the IRS are quite the opposite: As the taxpayer, you bear the burden of proving that what you did was correct. The IRS rarely has to prove its position. Is this fair? No. Frustrating? Absolutely. But adopting an adversarial posture won't help.

In Chapter 8, we will talk specifically about corresponding in writing with the IRS. Keep these points in mind for your overall dealings with the IRS, whether it's in writing, on the phone, or in person:

Be Courteous and Adopt a Collaborative Attitude

Employees at the IRS work at their jobs every day just like you—and, just like you, they want to be treated with respect and courtesy when they're working. Are you motivated to go out of your way to help someone who is rude and hostile? Not likely—so why would someone who works at the IRS be any different? Chances are, the IRS worker who answers the phone when you call or opens your letter when you write did not cause your problem. You may have very strong feelings about the agency in general and your situation in particular, but taking it out on a single individual isn't going to help and will probably hurt. The IRS employee who is handling your case is not the source of your troubles but they just may be the solution. And even if the person you are dealing with did make a mistake and cause a problem, it will still be to your advantage to take a positive and polite approach.

Timeliness and Responsiveness Are Critical

When you receive a written or telephone inquiry from an IRS representative, it is important that you respond promptly. The reason for the inquiry will not disappear if you just ignore it. You will be repeatedly contacted until you respond—and the longer you take, the worse matters will get.

Keep Track of Your Contacts

Maintain records of every contact you have with the IRS, whether by mail or on the phone. Record the date, the issue you discussed, the method of contact, the name and ID number of the person with whom you spoke, and what the two of you agreed the next step should be. You need a thorough, sequential record so you will have the answers you need if a question arises, and you will likely refer to these records time and time again. Remember, it is not the IRS' job to keep up with every aspect of your case—that's your responsibility. See page 95 in Chapter 8 for a sample IRS Communication Record.

Be Clear, Concise, and Neat

No matter how frustrated you are or how much of a hurry you are in, all of the documents you prepare for the IRS should be well organized and legible. It's highly likely as you work through the process of resolving your tax issues that you'll be asked to provide the same information or the same paperwork repeatedly. Don't be tempted to rush through it because you've done it before and you're annoyed.

It's not going to help your case if an IRS employee has to take a lot of time to decipher your handwriting or guess at what you're reporting. Don't give them a reason to come back to you with more questions—or worse, to misread or misunderstand you and respond to what they think you're telling them rather than to the actual facts.

When your financial forms and correspondence are messy and hard to read, the recipient is going to resent having to try to figure out the information and, worse, may also wonder if the information you're providing is indeed correct. After all, if you're sloppy when you fill out the form, it's not a leap to think that you may have also been sloppy when you gathered the information, and therefore the information may be incorrect. That's not the message you want to send to the IRS.

Before completing any IRS document, fill it out in draft form. If the IRS has sent you a document, make a copy of it for your draft. Most IRS forms can be downloaded at www.irs.gov, so you may be able to create your draft copy that way. Check, verify, and make any necessary corrections on the draft. Once you are satisfied that the information is complete and accurate, transfer the information to the final form as neatly and legibly as possible. If people tell you that your handwriting is hard to read, consider asking someone else to complete the form for you to sign.

The message you send when your work is neat, concise, precise, and well-documented is one of concern for accuracy and your willingness to cooperate, and your information will appear more believable and credible. The unwritten communication is that you know what you are doing and you are making every effort to resolve your problem.

> **TAX FACT**
> By law, the IRS can share your tax information with city and state tax agencies, and in some cases with the Department of Justice, other federal agencies, and people you authorize. The IRS can also share your tax information with certain foreign governments under tax treaty provisions.

Provide a Clear, Accurate, and Honest Picture of Your Finances

It's common for taxpayers to be tempted to slightly "fudge" the facts of their financial information. Their reasons range from fear of the IRS ("I don't want them to know how much I spend on _____") to reasons involving one's sense of self-worth ("I think my house should be valued higher than the other houses in the neighborhood") to an effort to hide resources in the hope that the IRS will not find and take them ("If the IRS doesn't know I have certain assets, it won't take them from me").

If you remember only one thing from this book, it should be this: *You must be absolutely truthful and forthcoming in all of your financial statements.*

When you are negotiating with the IRS, it is your responsibility to provide a clear, complete, accurate picture of your current financial condition. The IRS will verify all the information you provide, and trust me, you do not want to get caught lying to the IRS. You also do not want to give the impression that you are avoiding some issues or questions because that will cause the IRS agent to assume that you have something to hide, and he'll dig deeper to find out what that is. There is no better way to sabotage your work with the IRS than to be evasive or untruthful.

The other side of that coin is that you don't need to provide more information than is required by law. Some people are so frightened and intimidated by the IRS that they offer every detail, every paper, and every fact that may in any way affect their financial condition whether it is relevant to the issue at hand. IRS agents have plenty to do and they don't want to have to sort through a lot of extra "stuff." Keep your responses focused on the information that was requested.

Don't Work on Your Tax Problem When You Are Tired or Distracted

Most people find just reading a tax form difficult, frustrating, and confusing. Completing the actual form is often as difficult as reading

> **STAY OF COLLECTIONS**
>
> You may request a temporary delay in collection activity, known as a Stay of Collections, which is when you ask the IRS to hold off on enforced collection activity for a short period (up to 90 days) to allow you time to file returns, gather information, or make your own payment arrangements (such as securing a loan) before a levy is issued. If the stay is granted, the IRS will not contact you about your back taxes during that period. Just remember that this is a very short-term period, so make good use of this time.

the instructions. That's why you should not try to work on your tax problem when you are tired or don't have sufficient time to devote to the task. At the same time, I repeat that missing deadlines and failing to respond can seriously hurt your case. If you are going to handle your tax problem yourself, commit sufficient time and resources to do it right.

Utilize IRS Resources

The IRS has a number of resources for taxpayers to use at no charge. The most comprehensive is the IRS website at www.irs.gov. You may also call the IRS for live assistance Monday through Friday from 7:00 a.m. to 10:00 p.m. or call for recorded assistance 24 hours a day. Or you may visit your nearest Taxpayer Assistance Center for a face-to-face meeting.

What Are Your Options?

Now that you understand how the IRS collection process works and how to deal with the agency, it's time to look at your options for resolving your tax problem. There are only four ways to discharge your tax obligation to the federal government. Each of these options is associated with certain conditions, criteria, and obligations. There are advantages and disadvantages to each which may or may not apply to you in your particular situation. Let's take an overview look at each one (we'll go into greater detail in later chapters):

GUIDELINES FOR BORROWING FROM A RELATIVE

If you decide to settle your tax debt by borrowing the money you owe the government from a friend or relative, these tips will help you secure the funds you need while preserving your personal relationship with the lender:

- Only borrow money the lender is not likely to need in the foreseeable future and can afford to do without or lose if something happens and you are unable to repay the loan on schedule.
- Offer and expect to pay reasonable interest on the money you borrow.
- Put the complete loan agreement in writing and have all parties sign it. This eliminates the possibility of misunderstandings as to the terms and provides a degree of security for the lender if you default on the loan.

Full Pay

You can pay the entire amount you owe, plus whatever interest and penalties have accrued, and the matter is closed. I realize that for most people this is easier said than done, but it's worth exploring. The benefit is that the interest and penalties will stop, liens (if any) will be lifted, and your interaction with the IRS will be reduced to your annual tax return filing. If you don't have the cash on hand, consider borrowing it. You may be able to put it on a credit card (yes, the IRS accepts credit card payments); borrow from a traditional lender (difficult in today's credit environment); or borrow from a friend or relative. If you have a retirement account or life insurance with a cash value, consult with a qualified financial advisor before deciding to use funds from those sources to pay your tax debt; it may or may not be advisable depending on the totality of your circumstances.

Installment Agreement

If your financial situation is such that you do not have a lump sum of cash available to pay your taxes but you have income above what the IRS considers basic living expenses, you will be expected to use that income to pay your tax obligation. There are two types of installment agreements you can negotiate with the IRS: One is to pay off your tax debt in full over a certain period of time. While you are making payments, interest and penalties will continue to accrue on the unpaid balance.

The other is essentially a hybrid of an installment agreement and an offer in compromise, where you pay a monthly amount over the period of time remaining under the statue of limitations and the IRS will accept that as payment in full and discharge the unpaid liability, even though the total amount you'll end up paying is less than the total amount due. We'll discuss both types of installment agreements in greater detail in Chapter 7.

Offer in Compromise

This is the option that many tax representation services are referring to when they talk about settling your tax debt for a fraction of what you owe. The Offer in Compromise (OIC) program allows a taxpayer to make an offer to settle a tax debt for less than what is owed, wipe the slate clean, and get a fresh start.

The most important thing to recognize about the offer in compromise is that only a small percentage of taxpayers qualify for it. You can't just write the IRS a letter saying, "I know I owe you $100,000 in back taxes, interest, and penalties. How about if I pay you $10,000 and we call it even?" You must prove to the IRS that you have so little in negotiable assets and anticipated income beyond living expenses that there is no reasonable way in the foreseeable future that you will be able to pay off your tax debt completely. You may also use the OIC program if you believe you do not owe what the IRS says you owe. We'll discuss the three types of offers available under the OIC program in Chapter 6.

Currently Not Collectible

If you have no negotiable assets or income—for example, if you are unemployed and have exhausted your savings—the IRS may declare your case to be currently not collectible (CNC). Being currently not collectible doesn't mean the debt goes away. It means that the IRS has determined you cannot currently afford to pay the debt and there's nothing to be gained by pursuing you at this time so enforced collection activity ceases. However, penalties and interest will continue to be added to the debt while it is in CNC status and the IRS may file a Notice of Federal Tax Lien to make sure you don't sell any of your assets without considering the tax debt. If your financial situation doesn't change, your account can stay in this status until the statute of limitations runs out and then it will be written off. However, if your circumstances change and the IRS believes you have the resources to pay your tax obligation, it can move your account out of CNC and into collections.

Your request to be placed in CNC status must be submitted with the appropriate financial forms and documentation supporting your claim. The IRS doesn't just take your word for it—you must prove it. You should complete Form 433A Collection Information Statement (discussed in more detail in Chapter 6) and attach your supporting documents.

TAX FACT

The law allows the IRS to contact third parties as part of investigating your case. Those third parties include other people and entities, such as your neighbors, banks, employers, or employees. You have the right to request a list of third parties contacted with respect to your case.

You don't have to stay in CNC status if you are able to pay your tax debt and want to get the situation resolved before the statute of limitations runs out. You can request an installment agreement or submit an offer in compromise while you are in CNC or after the IRS changes your status. It would be highly unusual for the IRS to accept an installment agreement if you are unable to show the ability to pay, but it's possible.

IRS Collection Notices

The particular collection notice (or notices) that you receive from the IRS will indicate how much you owe and the applicable tax years.

You may receive several copies of the same notice issues for each separate tax year that is outstanding. Most notices request immediate payment of the full liability, which is likely not feasible and which is why you need to respond to the notice by the indicated deadline.

IRS collection notices will always be dated and include your taxpayer identification number, the tax form and year the notice concerns, the amount owed (if applicable), and IRS contact information. Let's take a look at the most common types of collection notices (note that the notice numbers are subject to change):

L3172 Notice of Federal Tax Lien Filing. This tells you a lien has been filed and explains your appeal rights. The lien is filed in the county where the taxpayer resides. This does not actually take any property or income; it merely protects the IRS' interest in any property should you want to sell, refinance, or otherwise dispose of the property before your tax obligation is satisfied.

Form 668Y Notice of Federal Tax Lien. This form is filed in the county courthouse as public record. The notice is actually a copy of the lien that has been filed.

L2801 Change in Withholding. This form tells you that the IRS has adjusted your W-4 withholding amount. Notice is also sent to your employer. Typically this action is taken when the IRS determines that the amount being withheld from your wages is not sufficient to meet your tax obligations. This is not a levy and can't be changed except by subsequent action by the IRS.

CP515 Request for Your Tax Return. This is your notification that the IRS has no return on record for you for the specified period. You are advised to immediately file the return and pay any tax due or, if you have already filed the return, to submit a copy of it.

L112 Notice of Payment or Credit. The IRS has payments reported for a period in which a return has not been filed. This does not mean you are entitled to a refund because the tax liability is undetermined until a return is filed. What the IRS wants you to do is either file a return or, if the payment report is inaccurate, take steps to correct it.

L2566 Proposed Individual Income Tax Assessment. When you have not filed a return, the IRS completes a substitute for return (SFR), calculates your tax, interest, and penalties for you based on income only and notifies you with this letter.

CP22 We Changed Your Return. This informs you that the IRS has made corrections to a return that will result in either a refund or additional tax due. When the change creates an additional tax liability, it is usually because of under- or unreported income or a math error. If the adjustments are accurate and not appealed, any resulting liability is valid.

CP14 Request for Payment. This notifies you of an outstanding balance. The due date in this notice is the deadline to prevent additional penalties and interest, not to prevent a levy.

CP49 Overpaid Tax Applied to Other Taxes You Owe. This tells you that any tax you may have overpaid is being applied to your outstanding tax liability. For example, if you owe back taxes for 2007 but are due a refund for 2010, that refund will be applied to what you owe for 2007 instead of being sent to you. Payments are applied to the oldest liability first. If all liabilities are satisfied by the overpaid tax, any amount remaining will be refunded. Refunds applied to an outstanding liability cannot be retrieved.

CP501 Reminder. This reminds you that you have a balance due and advises that the IRS may file a lien and that additional penalties and interest will accrue if the amount due is not paid within 10 days. This is not a levy deadline.

CP71 Reminder of Taxes Due. This notifies you of an outstanding balance. The due date provided is to prevent additional penalties and interest; it is not a levy deadline.

CP503 Important Notice. This is a computer-generated notice issued prior to the intent to levy and notifies you of an outstanding balance.

CP504 Intent to Levy. This requests payment within 10 days to avoid additional penalties and interest; however, despite the name of this notice, it does not actually indicate that you will be levied in 10 days.

CP92 Notice of Levy on Your State Tax Refund. This tells you that the IRS has seized a state-issued refund.

CP521 Monthly Statement. If you are on an installment payment plan, this notice will advise the current status of your account.

CP523 Defaulted Installment Agreement. If you are on an installment plan, this notice is usually issued because you have ceased making payments or have accrued an additional liability (which would be considered in default on the agreement that requires you to remain current on filing tax returns and on all new tax liabilities). This notice provides 30 days to reinstate the previous arrangement, after which the IRS may levy a state tax refund and/or file a lien.

L1058 Final Notice of Intent to Levy. This notice indicates the IRS has identified an asset it intends to levy. The next notice will be levy instructions directed to your employer, bank, or receivables.

CP91 Final Notice Before Levy on Social Security Benefits. This notice tells you that the IRS will issue a levy against 15 percent of your Social Security benefits (including Social Security disability benefits) in 30 days if you do not pay or make arrangements to pay your balance due.

Actual levy notices are sent directly to the levying source (such as your employer or bank), not to the taxpayer. We'll discuss this in detail in Chapter 5.

> **RESPECTFULLY QUOTED**
> "I owe the government $3,400 in taxes. So I sent them two hammers and a toilet seat."
> —Michael McShane

When You Paid but the IRS Says You Didn't

As is the case with just about every creditor, there will be times when payments to the IRS go astray and you really did pay the taxes the IRS claims you didn't. If you receive a notice demanding payment for taxes you have already paid, the first step is to check your own records and confirm that the payment was in fact made and, if you paid by check, that the check was cashed. It's usually a simple matter to respond to the notice with an affidavit stating the date of payment, how the payment was made (paper check, electronic transfer, money order, cashier's check, credit card), and any other evidence such as a copy of the canceled check or a bank or credit card statement showing the transaction.

Following these tips will reduce the risk of your payments to the IRS being lost or misapplied:

- Always use an easily traceable payment device, such as a check drawn on your own bank account, a bank cashier's check (not a money order), or a credit card.
- Write your name as it appears on your tax return, your Social Security number, and the tax period for which the payment is being made on the payment device.
- If you're including a payment with your return, complete Form 1040-V (payment voucher) and enclose that in the envelope along with your return and payment. If you are making a payment in response to another notice that included a payment stub, detach the stub and return it with your payment. You may also write a cover letter explaining what the payment is for; be sure that your cover letter has your full name as it appears on your tax return as well as your Social Security number.
- If you're paying on more than one account, use separate payment devices. Send each payment in a separate envelope—the small cost of the extra postage is worth it. And never combine business and personal tax payments.
- If you're mailing your payment, use certified mail with return receipt requested so that you are notified when your envelope is received by the IRS.

Statute of Limitations

The IRS has three years to issue a refund, three years to audit your tax return, and 10 years to collect any tax due. In other words, if the

IRS doesn't manage to collect your back taxes within 10 years, the debt disappears. This is what we mean when we refer to the statute of limitations. The clock on the statute of limitations starts running when the tax is assessed.

The 10-year collection period is suspended while the IRS and Office of Appeals consider a request for an installment agreement or offer in compromise; from the date you request a Collection Due Process (CDP) hearing until a Notice of Determination is issued or until the tax court's decision becomes final; from the date you request innocent spouse relief until a final Notice of Determination is issued; for tax periods included in a bankruptcy while the automatic stay is in effect, plus an additional six months; and while you are residing outside the United States, if you are absent for a continuous period of at least six months. The amount of time the suspension is in effect will be added to the time remaining in the original 10-year period.

Prior to the IRS Restructuring and Reform Act of 1998, the IRS could—and did—automatically extend the 10-year statute of limitations on collections for an additional 10 years without your consent. Now the statute of limitations cannot be extended without your consent. There may be times when you are negotiating a settlement of some sort when you'll want to consider agreeing to extend the statute of limitations. Give this a lot of serious thought and consult with a professional to be sure you understand all your options and the consequences.

Here's a classic example of the statute of limitations working to the advantage of a taxpayer. In 2000, I had a client—a brother and sister who owned a restaurant—who owed about $300,000 in payroll taxes that they couldn't afford to pay in full. The restaurant had failed and the IRS had assessed the owners personally for those unpaid taxes. We made two offers in compromise over a three-year period, which the IRS refused. At that point, there were only four years left on the statute of limitations for that debt. After refusing my clients' offers in compromise, the IRS ceased active collections. The statute of limitations expired and now my clients are free of that debt.

Let me be very clear on this: If you have the ability and resources to pay, you cannot choose to not pay your taxes and wait for the statute of limitations to run out. That's tax evasion, and it will likely lead to criminal charges. But if you legitimately do not have the resources to pay, the statute of limitations serves as a vehicle to give you a fresh start after a period of time, much like the bankruptcy code does for other debts.

Now that you know how to deal with the IRS and what your basic options are, let's go into more detail about what you can do to resolve your tax situation.

HIGHLIGHTS

- The first step in resolving your back tax issues is making the decision to take action.
- Whether you handle your back tax problems yourself or hire a professional to represent you is a decision only you can make after you have analyzed your situation.
- Before you can resolve your tax problems, you must first know exactly how much you owe and be in compliance with IRS regulations. This means getting your tax returns filed, even if you can't afford to pay what you owe.
- Electronic filing is available for the current year's tax return only. Previous years must be filed on paper.
- When filing past due returns, don't skip any years. Start with the oldest and file them in order at the same time.
- File each return in a separate envelope sent by certified mail, return receipt requested.
- You have rights as a taxpayer; take the time to understand what those rights are and how to exercise them.
- When working with the IRS, be courteous and adopt a collaborative attitude; remember that timeliness and responsiveness are critical; keep track of your contacts; be clear, concise, and neat; provide a

clear, accurate, and honest picture of your finances; don't work on your tax problems when you are tired or distracted; and utilize the resources the IRS provides.
- Your options for dealing with back taxes are: full pay; installment agreement; offer in compromise; currently not collectible.
- Borrowing money to pay a back tax debt can be a good option. If you borrow from a relative, be sure the lender can afford to be without the money for the time it will take you to repay it and treat the loan as a business transaction with clear terms and interest.
- As with any creditor, there is always a chance that the IRS will lose or misapply your payments. Always use an easily traceable payment device, mark it clearly with your full name and Social Security number, and enclose the proper documentation.
- The IRS has three years to issue a refund, three years to audit your tax return, and 10 years to collect any tax due.

4

What You Need to Know About Interest and Penalties

It's important that you understand the difference between interest and penalties, including when and how each is assessed. These add-ons can turn a reasonable tax bill into an astronomical obligation. IRS penalties and interest assessments are designed to get your attention and make you want to pay your liability before it gets even larger.

By definition, interest is the fee charged to a borrower by a lender for the use of borrowed money. When you owe money to the IRS, you have essentially borrowed that money from the government and you will be charged interest on the amount you owe until it is paid.

The general definition of penalty is a punishment, a payment for not fulfilling a contract, or the painful consequences of an action or condition. Most IRS penalties result from the inaction (which is in itself a type of action) of the taxpayer. The Internal Revenue Code imposes many different kinds of penalties, ranging from civil fines to imprisonment for criminal tax evasion. You may be assessed a penalty for failing to file your return and pay your taxes on time. Penalties may also be charged if you substantially understate your tax liability, understate a reportable transaction, file an erroneous claim for refund or credit, file a frivolous tax submission, or provide fraudulent information on your return.

Some penalties may be abated (reduced or canceled) if you have reasonable cause. Interest charges are generally not abated and they will continue to accrue until all assessed tax, penalties, and interest are paid in full. The only time an interest charge is adjusted is if the penalty is abated; in that case, the IRS will also reverse the interest charged on the abated penalty.

The deadline for most people to file their individual income tax returns and pay any tax owed is April 15. You can file for an extension to delay filing your actual return, but you must pay whatever tax you owe by April 15 to avoid interest and penalties.

Tax returns are checked for mathematical accuracy and then, if any money is owed to the government, you will receive a bill. Interest is charged on any unpaid tax from the due date of the return until the date of the payment. The interest rate is the federal short-term rate plus 3 percent; it is determined quarterly and compounded daily.

If you file your return on time but don't pay all of the tax due, you'll be charged a late payment penalty of one-half of 1 percent of the tax owed for each month, or part of a month, that the tax remains unpaid from the due date, until the tax is paid in full or the 25 percent maximum penalty is reached. And if you need another reason to always open and respond to correspondence from the IRS, here it is: The one-half of 1 percent rate increases to 1 percent if the tax remains unpaid 10 days after the IRS issues a notice of intent to levy.

There are also good reasons to file your return on time, even if you can't pay the tax. If you enter into an installment agreement to pay the tax due and you file your return by the due date, the one-half of 1 percent rate decreases to one-quarter of 1 percent for any month in which an installment

TAX FACT

If you are unable to pay your entire tax bill when it is due, pay as much as you can so that you reduce the amount of interest and penalties that will be assessed on the past due amount.

What You Need to Know About Interest and Penalties   45

agreement is in effect. If you owe tax and don't file on time, the total late-filing penalty is usually 5 percent of the tax owed for each month or part of a month that your return is late, up to 5 months or until the 25 percent maximum penalty is reached.

YOU MAY HAVE TO PAY CIVIL PENALTIES FOR ...

- **Filing late.** A failure-to-file penalty may be assessed if you do not file your return by the due date (including extensions). Additional penalties may be assessed if you file more than 60 days late or if your failure to file is due to fraud. If you can show that you failed to file on time because of reasonable cause and not because of willful neglect, you should not have to pay the penalty.
- **Paying tax late.** If your taxes are not paid by the due date, you will be charged a failure to pay penalty. If a notice of intent to levy or a notice and demand for immediate payment is issued, the penalty rate increases.
- **Failing to make appropriate estimated tax payments.** If you receive income from which taxes are not withheld, you must make estimated tax payments in a sufficient amount and on the correct schedule, or you may have to pay a penalty.
- **Providing inaccurate information.** If you underpay your tax because you substantially understate your income tax or show negligence or disregard of the rules and regulations, you may have to pay an accuracy-related penalty. The term "negligence" includes a failure to make a reasonable attempt to comply with the tax law, to exercise ordinary and reasonable care in preparing a return, or failure to keep adequate books and records.
- **Filing an erroneous claim for refund or credit.** You may have to pay a penalty if you file a claim for a refund or credit that is disallowed.
- **Filing a frivolous tax submission.** Frivolous tax returns or other submissions are subject to a penalty of $5,000. A frivolous tax return is one that does not include enough information to figure the correct tax or that contains information clearly showing that the tax you reported is substantially incorrect.
- **Civil fraud.** If any underpayment of tax on your return was due to

fraud, a civil penalty of 75 percent of the underpayment will be added to your tax debt.
- **Failure to supply your Social Security number (SSN).** If you do not include your SSN or the SSN of another person where required on a return, statement, or other document, you are subject to a penalty of $50 for each failure. This penalty also applies if you don't provide your SSN to another person or entity that needs it for a return, statement, or other document.
- **Bouncing a check to the IRS.** If you pay your taxes with a check and the check bounces, the IRS may impose a penalty.

YOU MAY BE SUBJECT TO CRIMINAL PROSECUTION FOR ...
- **Tax evasion.**
- **Willful failure** to file a return, supply information, or pay any tax due.
- **Fraud and false statements.**
- **Preparing and filing a fraudulent return.**

Reducing or Abating Penalties

Often it is the interest and penalties applied to an original tax liability that sinks a taxpayer so deep that they can never hope to climb out of the financial hole into which they have fallen. As you've already learned, the interest rate is the federal short-term rate plus 3 percent; it is determined quarterly and compounded daily. That means that interest is calculated and applied to your balance today; then tomorrow, interest will be calculated and applied to that balance, so you are paying interest on the interest. Some penalties can be as can be as high as 50 percent of the original liability. The goal of the IRS is to make it so painful for not filing your returns or paying your taxes on time that you are motivated to do it.

With that said, there are certain circumstances under which the IRS will reduce or abate (dismiss) a penalty. While it rarely adjusts interest charges, it is somewhat more flexible with penalties. The six reasons the IRS will consider reducing or abating penalties are:

What You Need to Know About Interest and Penalties 47

1. Death or serious illness of the taxpayer or a death or serious illness in his or her immediate family. In the case of a corporation, estate, trust, etc., the death or serious illness must have been of an individual having sole authority to execute the return or make the deposit or payment.

> **RESPECTFULLY QUOTED**
>
> "Next to being shot at and missed, nothing is really quite as satisfying as an income tax refund."
>
> —F. J. Raymond

2. Unavoidable absence of the taxpayer. In the case of a corporation, estate, trust, etc., the absence must have been of an individual having sole authority to execute the return or make the deposit or payment.
3. Destruction by fire or other casualty of the taxpayer's place of business or business records.
4. Taxpayer was unable to determine the amount of deposit or tax due to reasons beyond the taxpayer's control. However, this cause will be acceptable for taxpayers required to make deposits or payments of trust fund taxes only when the taxpayer was unable to have access to his or her own records.
5. The taxpayer's ability to make deposits or payments has been materially impaired by civil disturbances.
6. Lack of funds is an acceptable reasonable cause for failure to pay any tax or make a deposit under the Federal Tax Deposit System only when a taxpayer can demonstrate that the lack of funds occurred despite the exercise of ordinary business care and prudence.

The IRS will consider other explanations of situations where you can show you exercised ordinary business care and prudence but were delinquent in filing returns or making deposits or payments through circumstances beyond your control. Your reasons for filing late, providing inaccurate information, or not sending in payments on schedule should be concurrent with the seriousness of the above reasons. In other words, a life-altering crisis such as death, serious illness, fire, loss or destruction of records, natural disaster, or civil disturbance is considered "reasonable cause" to abate penalties.

There are two components to making a successful abatement request. One, you must provide a complete, thorough, and comprehensive explanation of what happened. Two, you must supply documentary evidence supporting your explanation. Support documentation might include newspaper clippings that show death, disaster, or civil disturbance; doctor statements or hospital records that show illness or injury; photographs; notarized statements from witnesses; or government records.

The IRS considers each abatement request individually. Some of the things that will affect the ultimate decision are:

- The quality, clarity, and comprehensiveness of your explanation.
- The quality and amount of supporting documentation substantiating your claim.
- Your efforts to correct the situation as it occurred and after it occurred.
- Your efforts to keep the situation from happening or to resolve the adverse tax consequences of the situation.
- Your reputation and history as a taxpayer.

HIGHLIGHTS

- Know the difference between interest and penalties. Interest is the fee charged by a lender (and when it comes to back taxes, the IRS essentially functions as a lender) for the use of borrowed money. Penalties are designed to be punishment and are charged when you fail to file your returns and pay your taxes in accordance with IRS rules.
- The IRS almost never cancels or reduces interest charges on assessed tax. Penalties may be reduced or abated under certain circumstances and if that happens, any interest charged on the penalties that are reduced or abated will be adjusted accordingly.

What You Need to Know About Interest and Penalties   49

- You may have to pay civil penalties for filing late; paying tax late; failing to make estimated tax payments; providing inaccurate information; filing an erroneous claim for refund or credit; filing a frivolous tax submission; civil fraud; failing to provide your social security number; and bouncing a check to the IRS.
- You may be subject to criminal prosecution for tax evasion; willful failure to file a return, supply information, or pay any tax due; committing fraud and making false statements; and preparing and filing a fraudulent return.
- The IRS considers each request for penalty reduction and/or abatement individually.

5

Understanding Liens and Levies

A key to understanding the consequences of back tax debt is understanding liens and levies. A *lien* is a legal claim against property, whether personal or real property (real estate), that essentially makes it collateral for a debt. A *levy* is a legal seizure of your property to satisfy a tax debt. They are distinctly different collection actions.

If a lien has been filed against your property (such as your home, car, or boat), you still own the property, but the lien must be satisfied before ownership of the property can be transferred. For example, if you have a federal tax lien against your home, you must pay the tax debt before you can sell that home. But you can continue to live in the home even though the property has a lien against it.

In the case of a levy, the government actually takes the property. If the property is cash, the amount is applied to your tax debt; personal or real property will be sold and the proceeds applied to your tax debt. Wage garnishment is a form of levy where the IRS takes a portion of your salary to satisfy your tax debt.

Something else the IRS can do that's similar to a levy is called *offset*. If you have overpaid your taxes for one tax period but owe taxes for another, the IRS can apply any refund you might be due on the overpayment to the unpaid tax—your debt is offset by your refund.

The Federal Tax Lien Process

A federal tax lien is a claim against your property—all of your property, including what you acquire after the lien arises (after it comes into existence). The lien arises automatically when you fail to pay the taxes you owe within 10 days after the IRS sends out the first notice. This is a statutory lien; it is created by the statutes when you fail to pay. At this point, the federal tax lien is a "silent lien," which means nobody knows about it except the IRS and you. A silent lien is still a valid lien and something you need to be concerned about; it's just not public information.

After a federal tax lien arises, the IRS may file a Notice of Federal Tax Lien in the public records at the county courthouse where you live or own property. When this happens, your creditors can easily find out that the federal government has a claim against all your property as well as to all of your rights to property, such as the accounts receivable of your business. Usually credit bureaus discover this information when they do their routine updates, so you can expect a federal tax lien to appear on your credit reports within a fairly short period of time after it is filed in the public records. This will affect your credit rating and make it difficult and maybe even impossible to get a loan, buy a house or car, or sign a lease.

Generally, a lien will release automatically 10 years after a tax is assessed, as long as the government has not filed it again or issues a Certificate of Release of Federal Tax Lien. The latter will be issued within 30 days after the IRS determines that the debt (tax plus accrued interest and penalties) has been satisfied, either by paying the debt or having it adjusted, or within 30 days after the IRS accepts a bond submitted by the taxpayer guaranteeing payment of the debt.

Understanding Liens and Levies

Keep in mind that the amount shown on the Notice of Federal Tax Lien is the unpaid balance on the date the notice is created. The notice will not be updated to show changes in the amount you owe—both increases due to interest and penalties and/or decreases due to payments. If you want to know the current lien payoff amount, you have to contact the IRS. If you sell property that is subject to a tax lien or pay your tax liability equal to the value of the property secured by the tax lien, you may apply for a Certificate of Discharge, which requests the release of the lien against that one piece of property.

If you owe back taxes, the silent lien exists. It is in your best interest to do everything possible to avoid the filing of the public Notice of Federal Tax Lien.

Getting a Federal Tax Lien Released

Once your tax debt has been paid in full, satisfied through an offer in compromise or an installment agreement, the IRS has accepted bond that the taxpayer submits, or the statute of limitations expires, the IRS must issue a certificate of lien release within 30 days. Understand that simply getting an offer in compromise (OIC) or an installment agreement (IA) accepted will not get a lien released; you must completely satisfy the terms of the OIC or IA. The process is supposed to be automatic, but it's a good idea for you to follow up to make sure it does.

If the lien has not been released after 30 days, contact the IRS Lien Processing Unit. Be prepared to play a game of phone tag; this can take a while, but your persistence will ultimately pay off. If you can't get the Lien Processing Unit to take the appropriate action or if you are in a time-sensitive situation (such as if you're trying to close on a mortgage), contact the Taxpayer Advocate Service for assistance.

Self-Releasing Liens

A lien usually releases automatically 10 years after a tax is assessed if the statutory period for collection has not been extended and the

> **TAX FACT**
> Contact information for the IRS Lien Processing Unit:
> Internal Revenue Service
> Lien Processing Unit
> Stop 8420G
> P.O. Box 145595
> Cincinnati, OH 45250-5595
> (800) 913-6050

IRS extended the effect of the lien by re-filing it. When a lien is self-released, the Notice of Federal Tax Lien itself is the release document. You should check the column titled "Last Day for Re-filing" on the Notice of Federal Tax Lien to determine if the lien is self-releasing and if it has indeed self-released.

You may want to request a certificate of release even when the lien is self-releasing, because creditors may not be willing to consider the self-releasing language on the Notice of Federal Tax Lien when evaluating you for credit. While this isn't essential, it can be helpful if you're working on cleaning up your credit record or are applying for a loan.

> **TAX FACT**
> If you believe a federal tax lien has been filed against you in error (which typically occurs when the name of the taxpayer is similar or identical to another person), you can request a Certificate of Nonattachment. See IRS Publication 1024: *How to Prepare Application for Certificate of Nonattachment of Federal Tax Lien.*

Withdrawal of Notice of Federal Tax Lien

The IRS rarely withdraws a federal tax lien, but it can happen. The circumstances under which the IRS will withdraw a filed Notice of Federal Tax Lien are:

- The notice was filed too soon or not according to IRS procedures.
- The taxpayer entered into an installment agreement to pay the debt described on the notice of lien (unless the installment agreement provides otherwise, which is often the case).
- Withdrawal would expedite collecting the tax.
- Withdrawal would be both in the taxpayer's best interest and in the best interest of the government.

Understanding Liens and Levies

SOCIAL SECURITY NUMBER (SSN) REDACTION FOR NOTICE OF FEDERAL TAX LIEN

The increasing problem of identity theft poses significant privacy concerns for public documents that include social security numbers and other personal information. This information has been used for many years on the public Notice of Federal Tax Lien.

In 2004, legislation was introduced in the U.S. House of Representatives that would have mandated elimination of full SSN information from publicly available documents. Although the legislation did not become law, the IRS decided to go forward with a plan to redact SSN information on the publicly recorded notice in a manner that conforms to the proposed federal legislation.

Effective January 2006, the Automated Lien System that generates lien filings was modified to include redacted SSN information in the format XXX-XX-NNNN. Only the last four digits will appear on the Notice of Federal Tax Lien. The last four digits may not be changed by the recording offices.

When a Notice of Federal Tax Lien is withdrawn, the IRS will provide a copy of the withdrawal and, if the taxpayer sends a written request, will send a copy to other institutions the taxpayer indicates.

IRS Tax Levies

As I've explained, levies are different from liens. Levies are the legal seizure of your property to satisfy a debt. If you do not pay your back taxes or make arrangements to settle the debt through an installment agreement or offer in compromise, the IRS can seize and sell property that you hold (such as your house, other real estate, car, or boat) or it can levy property that is yours but is held by someone else (such as your wages, retirement accounts, dividends, bank accounts, rental income, accounts receivables, the cash value of your life insurance, or commissions). The terms levy and garnishment are essentially interchangeable, but the IRS uses the term levy and states tend to use the term garnishment.

> **RESPECTFULLY QUOTED**
>
> "Mr. Gladstone, then Chancellor of the Exchequer, had interrupted him in a description of his work on electricity to put the impatient inquiry: 'But, after all, what use is it?' Like a flash of lightning came the response: 'Why, sir, there is every probability that you will soon be able to tax it!'"
>
> —Michael Farady

Levies will rarely come as a surprise. The IRS will typically levy only after the tax has been assessed and you have been sent a Notice and Demand for Payment, you have not paid the tax, and you have been sent a Final Notice of Intent to Levy and Notice of Your Right to a Hearing (levy notice) at least 30 days before the levy.

There are a number of circumstances under which a levy will be released. The most obvious, of course, is if you pay the taxes, penalties, and interest that you owe. The levy will be released if the IRS has made a mistake—for example, if it has not sent you the required notices or allowed the time required by law for you to respond, or if the levy is on property the IRS is not allowed to levy, or if you have an installment agreement in effect. The IRS may also release a levy if it determines that the expense of selling your property would be greater than the government's interest in the property or if it determines that the levy is creating an economic hardship for you. There are other circumstances under which a levy will be released, including if the IRS determines that doing so will help it collect the tax.

Once the IRS serves a levy on your wages, salary, commissions, or other payments for personal services, the levy continues until your tax debt is paid in full or other arrangements are made to satisfy the debt, or the time period for collecting expires.

The process is a little different when it comes to bank levies. You have 21 days after a levy is served before the IRS actually takes the funds, and during that time you have the opportunity to demonstrate hardship—for example, to show that if the IRS takes the money, you'll be evicted or your utilities will be disconnected. Another difference is that bank levies are essentially one-time actions. The levy

Understanding Liens and Levies

hits your bank, whatever is in your account is frozen, and those funds are transferred to the IRS 21 days later. If that amount did not satisfy your tax debt, the IRS has to issue another levy, which it won't do again for at least 30 days. Any funds that go through your account after the levy is issued are not affected by the levy.

This is what it would look like: Let's say you owe $5,000 in back taxes and have $1,000 in the bank. The IRS issues a levy for the $1,000 on March 1. On March 22, it takes the $1,000. In the meantime, on March 5, you received a paycheck for $2,000. That $2,000 is yours to use as you want and is not affected by the levy. By April 1, then, your tax debt has been reduced to $4,000 but you have $1,500 in the bank left over from what you were paid after the first levy was issued. The IRS can issue another levy on April 1; the $1,500 is frozen for 21 days and then taken by the IRS. But if you get paid again on April 5, that money won't be affected by the second levy. After the second levy, your tax debt has been reduced to $2,500. Understand that this example is very simplistic, because chances are if you are working and the IRS knows it, your wages will also be levied.

If you own a business, the IRS can levy your accounts receivable. That means that the IRS will notify your customers that instead of paying you, they must pay whatever they owe you to the IRS until your tax debt is satisfied. If your customers do not follow the instructions on the levy, they are subject to penalties.

Something that's very important to keep in mind is this: You will not be notified by the IRS of the actual levy. You'll get a notice of Intent to Levy that will include a telephone number you can call to make payment arranges to prevent the levy, but if you fail to take action on that intent to levy, the next communication from the IRS goes directly to your employer or the bank, not to you.

HIGHLIGHTS

- A lien is a legal claim against property that essentially makes it collateral for a debt; a levy is a legal seizure of property to satisfy a debt.

- A federal tax lien automatically arises when you fail to pay the taxes you owe within 10 days after the IRS sends out the first notice.
- A lien is considered "silent" (meaning that no one knows about it except you and the IRS) until the IRS files a Notice of Federal Tax Lien in the public records.
- A federal tax lien can be released once your tax debt has been paid in full, satisfied through an offer in compromise or an installment agreement, or the statute of limitations expires.
- A federal tax lien usually releases automatically after 10 years if the statutory period for collection has not been extended. This is known as a self-releasing lien.
- The IRS rarely withdraws a federal tax lien, but may do so under special circumstances.
- You will not be notified of an IRS levy. You will receive a Final Notice of Intent to Levy; the actual levy will be sent to your employer, bank, accounts receivables, or other entity.
- You have 21 days after a levy is served before the IRS takes the funds.

6

Offer in Compromise: Can You Really Settle for Less Than You Owe?

A compromise involves mutual concessions—both sides giving up part of what they want to reach an agreement that will bring a negotiation or situation to a close. The Offer in Compromise (OIC) program allows you to do that with your tax debt: you pay less than you owe and the IRS accepts that amount as payment in full and is able to close your case. While this sounds simple, it's not as easy as negotiating a "you pick the restaurant and I'll choose the movie" agreement with your spouse or partner.

I think it's safe to say that everyone who owes back taxes would like to settle their debt for less than they owe—but not everyone qualifies for an OIC. The program is only available under certain conditions and in certain situations. The IRS policy states:

> *The Service will accept an offer in compromise when it is unlikely that the tax liability can be collected in full and the amount offered reasonably reflects collection potential. ... The goal is to achieve collection of what is potentially collectible at the earliest possible time and at the least cost to the Government.*

In other words, the IRS wants to get as much as it possibly can of the amount you owe while spending the least amount in collection efforts. You've probably heard stories of people who have successfully negotiated an OIC for a mere fraction of what they owe. Do those cases really happen? Absolutely. Do they happen a majority of the time? No.

As you deal with the IRS on a back tax issue, keep this in mind: For the IRS, it's not about how much you owe, it's about how much you can pay. You are not eligible to request an offer in compromise if your liability can be paid by setting up an installment agreement, which we'll discuss in Chapter 7. If your monthly disposable income is sufficient to pay off your tax liability over the remaining time left on the Collection Statue of Limitations plus five years, you will not qualify for an OIC unless special circumstances exist. And the IRS doesn't just take your word for it when it comes to your ability or inability to pay. You have to provide complete documentation of your financial circumstances to justify your offer.

With that said, let's not assume that just because a small percentage of taxpayers are approved for an OIC that you couldn't be one of them. The OIC is still worth exploring because the process of determining whether or not you qualify for this program will also help you identify an alternate strategy for dealing with your tax debt if that becomes necessary.

Your offer package should consist of a cover letter, the appropriate IRS forms, and documentation supporting your position. The IRS forms you'll need to complete include Form 656 Offer in Compromise (or Form 565-L if you are filing based on doubt as to liability); Form 433-A, Collection Information Statement for Wage Earners and Self-Employed Individuals; and/or Form 433-B, Collection Information Statement for Businesses. Neither Form 433-A nor Form 433-B is required when your OIC is based on doubt as to liability.

The cover letter of your package—and indeed any letter you write to the IRS—should be carefully composed. It must be clear, easy to understand, and include all relevant facts and documentation. Because correspondence sent to the IRS is so critical, you should thoroughly study Chapter 8, which explains how to correspond with the IRS and includes some sample letters.

Let's begin with an overview of the three types of Offers in Compromise:

1. Doubt as to Collectibility
2. Doubt as to Liability
3. Effective Tax Administration

> **TAX FACT**
>
> IRS Policy P-5-100 issued in 1992 virtually created the tax representation industry. This policy states that the IRS will accept offers in compromise when it is unlikely that the tax liability can be collected in full and the amount offered reasonably reflects the collection potential. Tax professionals were able to add assisting clients with this process to their services and eventually firms began to specialize in representing taxpayers before the IRS.

Offer in Compromise—Doubt as to Liability

An Offer in Compromise—Doubt as to Liability is appropriate when you believe you do not owe what the IRS says you owe. You can file an offer based on doubt as to liability if you can show documentary evidence that questions the liability that was not available when the IRS first determined the amount of taxes owed.

This is the only kind of OIC that does not require full financial disclosure forms. Submitting an offer based on doubt as to liability only requires a letter of explanation about why you believe you do

> **OFFER IN COMPROMISE—DOUBT AS TO COLLECTIBILITY**
>
> The OIC based on doubt as to collectibility is the most frequently submitted of the three possible OICs. This offer is appropriate when you simply cannot pay what you owe the IRS within the remainder of the statutory period for collection. If you can prove that you have no assets to speak of and your income is only enough to cover basic living expenses as defined by the IRS, this type of offer is probably your best course of action.

not owe the liability along with the appropriate documentation to prove your case. Possible reasons to submit a Doubt as to Liability offer include: (1) the examiner made a mistake interpreting the law, (2) the examiner failed to consider the taxpayer's evidence, or (3) the taxpayer has new evidence. For example, let's say you took a substantial deduction for business expense that you could not document; you were audited and the IRS disallowed the deduction. After the IRS determined the amount of taxes owed, you located documentation to support your deduction. That would qualify you to file an offer based on doubt as to liability.

Offer in Compromise—Effective Tax Administration

An OIC filed under the conditions of Effective Tax Administration is usually reserved for serious hardship situation. You are not disputing the tax liability and you have the resources to pay it; however, you are in a situation where collection of the tax would create an economic hardship or would be unfair or inequitable. For example, let's say you have a dependent child who has a serious long-term illness for whom you provide full-time care and assistance. You have assets that could be liquated to pay your back taxes, but you know you are going to need the equity in those assets to provide basic care and pay medical expenses for your child. You are not disputing the tax debt; you are saying that to pay it would leave you unable to pay for the care your child needs. Other circumstances under which the IRS would consider an effective tax administration offer would be advanced age of the taxpayer, poor health, disability, or any situation where you can show potential economic hardship. You must also be able to show that the acceptance of such an

RESPECTFULLY QUOTED

"Of all debts men are least willing to pay the taxes. What a satire is this on government! Everywhere they think they get their money's worth, except for these."

—Ralph Waldo Emerson

offer would not be detrimental to voluntary compliance—that is, acceptance of the offer would not prevent you from voluntary compliance with tax laws.

Moving Forward with the Offer Process

If you believe that one of the OIC categories is applcable to your situation, you have a lot of work to do. We'll walk through the process in this chapter.

Begin with familiarizing yourself with all conditions and criteria under which your offer will be considered and/or accepted. A list of those required conditions and criteria is included in the checklist on page 64. Read it carefully. Some of the requirements should be resolved before you begin preparing your OIC. Other conditions on the list might automatically disqualify you—something you would want to know before you do a lot of work preparing your offer.

BASIC QUALIFICATION CRITERIA FOR OFFER IN COMPROMISE
- **Doubt as to Collectibility.** If the value of your assets and anticipated disposable income through the statutory collection period is less than your tax liability, you may qualify for this type of offer.
- **Effective Tax Administration.** If the value of your assets exceeds your total tax liability but you have special circumstances such as advanced age, diminishing earning capacity, or serious health problems, you may qualify for this type of offer.
- **Doubt as to Liability.** If you believe the amount assessed against you is incorrect and you have documents to support your belief, you could qualify for this type of offer.

OIC—Doubt as to Collectibility: Are You Eligible?

The first step in determining if you are eligible to submit an offer in compromise is to figure out whether or not you meet the basic requirements. It's actually much quicker and easier to find out if you are *not* qualified than it is to verify that you are. If you determine now that you are not eligible for the program, don't waste your time

OFFER IN COMPROMISE— GENERAL CONDITIONS AND CRITERIA CHECKLIST

- ❏ All tax returns have been filed with the IRS and are up to date.
- ❏ You are not currently involved in bankruptcy proceedings.
- ❏ You are willing and prepared to file and pay all taxes on time for at least the next five years.
- ❏ You are willing to keep the IRS informed of any change of location and/or address while you are paying off your liability.
- ❏ You are prepared to respond quickly and accurately to all inquiries or requests from IRS personnel regarding your OIC.
- ❏ You are willing to forfeit all present and future tax benefits while paying the liability agreed on in your offer.
- ❏ If you are currently paying your liability by an installment arrangement, you will continue paying regularly and on time throughout the OIC review process. (Exceptions to this condition may apply based on the terms of your offer.)
- ❏ You have some plan about how to pay the OIC if it is accepted by the IRS.
- ❏ Acceptance of your offer would not be detrimental to voluntary compliance and would not be in conflict with public policy.

submitting an offer—you will only delay a real resolution to your tax debt problems.

Whether you qualify to submit an offer based on doubt as to collectibility depends on two financial variables: the assets you own and the amount of income you regularly realize. Only taxpayers who have very little in assets and income will qualify for this type of OIC. It doesn't matter that you may have some very valid (to you) reasons for not wanting to dispose of certain assets to pay your taxes. Nor does it matter that you may want to maintain a certain standard of living that the IRS doesn't consider necessary. I know this may sound discouraging, but this is a point at which many of our clients need a serious reality check, and I want to give it to you as well.

As citizens and non-citizen residents of the United States of America, we are obligated to pay the taxes we owe. If you owe the government money and have not paid it, the IRS is going to find ways to collect that money. If you have possessions of any value (assets), the IRS will take those assets to apply to your tax liability. There are some assets the IRS won't go after (such as personal items, clothes, modest household furnishings), but they are few. The IRS will not force you to dispose of any assets during the OIC process, but will ask you to come up with an amount of cash equal to the equity in the asset.

Your disposable monthly income is also factored into the complex formula that determines eligibility to submit an OIC. Disposable monthly income is considered to be whatever remains after you pay your qualifying expenses. Qualifying expenses are those costs that the IRS has deemed allowable as essential to meet basic living requirements. Allowable expenses include food, shelter, utilities, transportation, and certain costs that are necessary for you to earn a living. The monthly income left after allowable basic expenses are paid is considered by the IRS to be disposable monthly income and, as such, is money available to be regularly applied against your tax debt.

Keep in mind that the IRS has its own standards for what constitutes basic living expenses. Regardless of how important these items might be to you, the IRS will typically not allow you to claim as qualifying expenses such items as tuition for private schools, public or private college expenses, charitable contributions, voluntary retirement contributions, payments on unsecured debts such as credit card bills, cable television charges, and other similar expenses. Exceptions may be made if you can prove an expense is necessary for the health and welfare of you or your family or for the production of income.

Is This an Option for You?

If you think you might be eligible for an OIC based on doubt as to collectibility based on what you've learned so far, this is a good time to do a short exercise. This won't produce an exact result that could provide a positive determination, but it will likely tell you quickly whether or not you are eligible for this type of OIC. It will give you a good sense of whether or not it's worth your time to pursue an OIC.

The worksheets on pages 67–69 will help you determine if you either absolutely do not qualify or if you might qualify for an OIC based on doubt as to collectibility.

Complete worksheets 1, 2, 3, and 4, filling in an approximate amount for each category that applies to you. Your best guesstimate for this exercise is sufficient; don't take the time at this point to research the precise numbers, but be honest. When you have completed all four worksheets, turn to the worksheet analysis form on page 70 to see if you might be eligible for an OIC or if that option has been ruled out.

If you find that you may qualify to submit an OIC, you need to do the detailed computations that will be necessary to definitively discover whether or not you actually qualify. Yes, this will be a lot of work, but once your information-gathering, paperwork, and calculations are done, you will not only know that you qualify for an OIC, you will also have finished assembling most of the information you will be required to send to the IRS with your application. In other words, by the time you learn whether or not you qualify, most of the hard work will be done. And if it turns out that you don't qualify for an OIC, you'll have the documentation you need to negotiate an installment agreement.

WORKSHEET 1

Income

Select the items that apply to your life situation and indicate the average monthly amount in the column on the right.

Income (salary—self) _____

Income (salary—spouse) _____

Investment income (self) _____

Investment income (spouse) _____

Child support _____

Alimony _____

Other business income _____

Retirement income _____

Other income _____

Total monthly income* $_____

*Note: For the purpose of an OIC, "income" does not mean just taxable income, but all sources of money coming into the household. Also, this is gross income before deductions.

WORKSHEET 2

Living Expenses

Select the items that apply to your situation and indicate the average monthly cost in the column on the right.

Rent or mortgage payment	_____
Utilities (gas, electricity, water, telephone, fuel oil, garbage) and housing (other than rent or mortgage)	_____
Transportation (car payments, gas, repairs, public transportation to work)	_____
Food	_____
Medical (prescriptions, OTC meds, doctor, dentist)	_____
Personal (clothing, personal care)	_____
Child/dependent care	_____
Taxes (federal, state, local, property)	_____
Court-ordered payments (alimony, child support)	_____
Total monthly expenses	$_____

WORKSHEET 3

Negotiable Assets
Select the items that apply to your situation and provide their approximate value in the column on the right.

Equity in your home (exclusive of any mortgage)	_____
Cash value of insurance policy or policies	_____
Investments (stocks, bonds, money market, mutual funds)	_____
Other property (cars, boat, motor home, etc.)	_____
Checking account balance	_____
Savings account balance	_____
Certificates of deposits	_____
Retirement accounts	_____
Education accounts	_____
Other accounts	_____
Other assets	_____
Total negotiable assets	$_____

WORKSHEET 4

Tax Liability
Add the total federal tax liability for all years and list that below.

Total tax liability owed $_____

WORKSHEET ANALYSIS

Fill in the blanks with the totals from the previous worksheets and follow the instructions.

Total from worksheet 1 (income)	$_____
Minus	
Total from worksheet 2 (expenses)	$_____
Equals	
Disposable monthly income	$_____

If the disposable monthly income is a negative number and the total on worksheet 3 is *less* than on worksheet 4, you may qualify for an OIC. Continue with the guidance in Chapter 6 for moving to the next step of the process.

If the disposable monthly income is a negative number and the total on worksheet 3 is *more* than on worksheet 4, you do not qualify for an OIC. Go to Chapter 7 for information on installment agreement options.

If the disposable monthly income is a positive number, work the following calculations:

Disposable monthly income	$_____
Multiply times 60*	
Equals	$_____
Plus	
Total from worksheet 3	$_____
Equals	$_____

If the above number is *less* than on worksheet 4, you may qualify for an OIC. Continue with the guidance in Chapter 6 for moving to the next step of the process.

If the above number is *more* than on worksheet 4, you don't qualify for an OIC. Go to Chapter 7 for information on installment agreement options.

*Note: The multiplier is 48 for a cash OIC; 60 for a short-term periodic payment or for the length of time remaining on the statute of limitations. Choose the multiplier that applies to your circumstances.

Compiling Your Financial Information

Before you begin the work of filling out the paperwork and calculating numbers, let's review what forms you're going to be working with and when each is required. You must use the most current version of all the IRS forms you file. The best source for these forms is www.irs.gov. You can also order forms to be sent to you through the mail by calling (800) 829-3676.

As explained at the beginning of this chapter, IRS Form 656 Offer in Compromise (or Form 656-L Offer in Compromise—Doubt as to Liability) is the form you use to submit an OIC. In most cases, you will also have to submit Form 433-A, Collection Information Statement for Wage Earners and Self-Employed Individuals, and/or Form 433-B, Collection Information Statement for Businesses. If your tax liability is business-related such that it's considered a corporate entity or a partnership, both the 433-A and 433-B will be required. If you are a wage earner or a sole proprietor, the 433-A will be sufficient. Neither the Form 433-A nor Form 433-B is required when a taxpayer submits an OIC based solely as to doubt as to liability.

Before you begin filling out the forms, gather all the financial information you're going to need. If you've ever worked on a project and had to repeatedly stop to get missing supplies or information, you know how frustrating such interruptions can be. For most people, working on a tax-related project is not pleasant, but you can keep the unpleasantness to a minimum by following this advice. Use the checklist on page 72 to make sure you have that information in one place before you tackle the forms. It's likely that gathering the information will be the longest and most tedious part of the entire process. You'll need to find old receipts, statements, and bills—and you're going to have to make copies of all those documents to attach to the Form 433-A or 433-B.

Set aside a full day to devote only to gathering the records you'll need to have at hand to prepare the financial forms

RESPECTFULLY QUOTED

"Income tax has made more liars out of the American people than golf."
—*Will Rogers*

required for your offer. Yes, this is monotonous and frustrating, but it's important. And it's something you're going to have to do whether you prepare your own OIC or retain a tax representation firm to do it for you. The IRS will want to see updated documentation throughout the OIC process, so this is a good time to get your financial paperwork in order so it's available when updated information is requested.

When you have your financial documents assembled, begin working on completing the 433-A and/or 433-B. These forms are user-friendly and self-explanatory. It's a good idea to get a draft copy of the forms for your working copy and then transfer the information to the final form you submit to the IRS when you have them complete.

CHECKLIST FOR GATHERING YOUR FINANCIAL RECORDS

Below is a list of many possible sources of financial information about you. Not all of the items on this list will apply to your situation. Read each description below and if it applies to you, stop and go get the applicable records for the number of months indicated. If you can't locate the exact type of record, look for any other document, receipt, or statement that reflects the same information. Once you have the papers in hand, check that particular item off the list. If an item on the list does not apply to you, put an X in the box next to the description. Continue gathering your records until you have completed the entire list.

❏ If you are self-employed, all invoices, commission statements, sales records, and/or income statements for the last three months.
❏ If you are an employee, all pay stubs and/or earnings statements for the last three months.
❏ If you have income from a pension fund, a statement or statements reflecting three months of income.
❏ If you receive income from Social Security, a statement or statements reflecting three months of income.
❏ If you receive income from a retirement fund, documents reflecting three months of income.
❏ Checking account statements (most current three months)

- ❏ Savings account statements (most current three months)
- ❏ Credit union account statements (most current three months)
- ❏ Brokerage account statements (most current three months)
- ❏ Money market account statements (most current three months)
- ❏ Savings account statements (most current three months)
- ❏ Proof of assets: Certificate of deposit and date of maturity
- ❏ Proof of assets: IRA
- ❏ Proof of assets: Keogh (date you will have access without penalty)
- ❏ Proof of assets: 401(k) (date you will have access without penalty)
- ❏ Proof of assets: Bonds (date of maturity)
- ❏ Proof of assets: Stocks
- ❏ Proof of assets: Mutual fund statement(s)
- ❏ Most recent statement for each credit card you own
- ❏ Whole life insurance statement
- ❏ Paperwork relative to any current lawsuits in which you are involved
- ❏ Paperwork relative to any legal judgments that you owe and/or are still paying
- ❏ Trust documents
- ❏ Documents pertaining to any transfers of assets *during the last 10 years*
- ❏ Documents pertaining to a profit sharing plan
- ❏ Car loan documents
- ❏ Notation of mileage for each automobile
- ❏ Car lease documents
- ❏ Loan documents or registration forms pertaining to any other licensed assets such as a boat, motorcycle, RV, truck, or automobile (specifically the make, model, year, and license number of each)
- ❏ Appraisal documents for any valuables you own
- ❏ Receipts for any business-related assets such as machinery or tools

Preparing and Submitting Your Offer

Once you have gathered your financial information and completed the financial forms, it's time to prepare your actual offer, which is Form 656. It's important that you read and understand every line on this form, even though much of it will sound familiar because you've read this book.

At this point, you will be expected to declare your preferred method of payment should your offer be accepted. You have one of three options available to you:

- **Cash:** The full amount offer is paid in cash or its equivalent in five or fewer installment payments on written notice of acceptance. Twenty percent of the OIC amount must be paid with the OIC submission as the down payment. The payment terms must be stated on the Form 656.

- **Short-term deferred:** The full amount offered is paid in more than six months but less than 24 months from the date of submission. The first payment must be submitted with your offer. Monthly payments are made while the OIC is in review.

- **Deferred payment:** The OIC amount is paid in monthly installments over the course of the latest statute of liability. The first payment must be submitted with your offer. Payments must be made during the OIC review.

How Much Should You Offer?

Deciding how much to offer in your OIC is not quite the same as negotiating to buy a used car. According to the IRS, your offer amount must equal or exceed your reasonable collection potential amount, and the information you provide on Forms 433-A and 433-B will assist the IRS in determining that figure. Essentially, it's the net equity of your assets plus the amount the IRS could collect from your future income. The IRS' Worksheet to Calculate an Offer Amount will help you use the information from Form 433-A to come up with your offer amount.

If you are making a cash offer and you will pay your installments in five months or less, you should offer the realizable value of your assets plus the total amount the IRS could collect over 48 months of payments or the remainder of the statutory period for collection, whichever is less. If the installments will be paid in more than five months but less than 24 months, you should offer the realizable value of your assets plus the total amount the IRS could collect over 60 months of payments. If it's going to take you more than 24 months to complete the five installment payments, you should offer the realizable value of your assets plus the total amount the IRS could collect over the number of months remaining on the statutory period for collection.

For a short-term deferred offer, the amount should include the realizable value of your assets plus any amount the IRS could collect over 60 months of payments or the remainder of the statutory period of collection, whichever is less. The amount of a deferred payment offer should include the realizable value of your assets plus the amount the IRS could collect through monthly payments during the remaining life of the collection statute.

Preparing Your Package

When you have completed all the necessary forms and attached the appropriate documentation, compose a cover letter to go with your package.

You will also need to include the application fee ($150 as of the date this book was written; contact the IRS to confirm the amount). You may request an exception to the application fee by completing Form 656-A. Offers submitted without either the application fee or a completed Form 656-A will not be processed.

You must also include what amounts to a good faith payment on the offer you are making. For lump sum cash payment offers, include 20 percent of the offer. If you are offering to make periodic payments, include the first installment of your payments. You may use Form 656-A to request an exception to this requirement if you

> **TAX FACT**
> When you fail to respond to an IRS notification that you owe taxes, the IRS acts on the assumption that the debt is valid and will take steps to collect the amount due.

qualify as low income by the IRS' standards. As with the application fee, offers submitted without a payment or a Form 656-A will not be processed.

If your offer is returned or not accepted, any fees and payments made with the filing of your offer will be applied to your outstanding tax liabilities.

What's Next?

Once the IRS receives your offer package, an examiner will evaluate it and may request additional documentation to verify the information you provided. Then the examiner will make a recommendation (which is essentially a preliminary decision) to accept or reject the offer. The examiner may also decide that a larger offer amount is necessary; if that happens, you'll be given the opportunity to amend your offer. For example, you may owe $25,000 and have offered $5,000 in cash to settle the debt. The examiner could come back and say that based on the information you provided, he believes you could pay $10,000. That's still a good offer—it's not the $5,000 you wanted to pay, but it's still substantially less than the $25,000 you owe.

If you fail to respond to the examiner's recommendation in 30 days, either by accepting it (which means you agree to whatever the examiner decides) or appealing it (which means you want them to either reconsider your original offer or you want to change your offer to one that is still less than the examiner's recommendation), your offer will be automatically rejected. If you appeal, you should provide additional documentation supporting your position with your appeal.

The IRS rarely accepts a taxpayer's first offer. This is not a negotiating ploy; it's because the IRS uses a math calculation based on your income, expenses, and how you value your assets. It's virtually impossible for any taxpayer to duplicate that calculation. But because of the way the IRS calculates offers, it is also possible—although not common—for the examiner to recommend an offer amount that's less than what you proposed.

The IRS will withhold collection activities while your offer is being investigated and considered; for 30 days after your offer is rejected; and while you appeal an offer rejection.

If your offer is accepted, you'll be notified by mail. At that point, you must promptly comply with all of the terms and conditions in your offer.

One of those terms will be to stay in compliance with future tax responsibilities (filing returns and paying current taxes) for five years. If you fail to do that, the IRS will reinstate the unpaid amount of the original tax liability, file a Notice of Federal Tax Lien on any tax liability without a filed notice, and resume collection activities.

If your OIC is rejected, you will have 30 days from the date of the notice to file an appeal to the rejection and supply additional information to support your position. An Appeals Officer will be in contact with you concerning your appeal. Like the review of your OIC, the appeals process may take several months.

HIGHLIGHTS

- The Offer in Compromise program allows taxpayers who qualify to pay less than what they actually owe to settle their tax debt.
- There are three types of offers: doubt as to collectibility; doubt as to liability; and effective tax administration.
- Doubt as to collectibility is the most commonly submitted type of offer and is appropriate when the taxpayer simply cannot pay what is owed within the remainder of the statutory period for collection.
- Doubt as to liability is appropriate when you believe you do not owe what the IRS says you owe.

- Effective tax administration does not dispute the tax or ability to pay, but is used when payment would create a serious hardship situation for the taxpayer.
- The IRS has clearly stated requirements to help taxpayers determine potential eligibility for a doubt as to collectibility offer. If you do not meet those requirements, your offer will be rejected.
- For most offers in compromise, you must submit full financial information. Set aside a full day to devote to gathering the records you'll need to prepare the financial forms the IRS requires.
- Your offer package should be prepared precisely according to the IRS' requirements and include a cover letter, application fee, and good faith payment.
- It may take months for the IRS to respond to your offer. When the IRS does respond, you will have 30 days to accept or appeal it, or the IRS will consider it rejected.

7

Installment Agreements: Paying Back Taxes Over Time

If you owe back taxes that you can't pay in a lump sum (or you don't want to have to liquidate assets to make an immediate lump sum payment) and you don't qualify to reduce the amount owed through an offer in compromise, you should be able to set up an installment agreement to pay the debt off over time.

As creditors go, the IRS is not going to be the warmest, friendliness entity you'll ever owe money to. The IRS isn't designed to be in the credit business and so it doesn't make it easy for you to owe back taxes or pay your tax obligation off over time. However, the government has come to recognize that there are circumstances when it must offer taxpayers alternatives to lump sum, on-time tax payments.

Installment agreements (IA) are generally available to all taxpayers and for all classes of tax with the basic requirements that you be current on all filing requirements and not have defaulted on a previous installment agreement. If you are not in compliance—that is, up to date with filing all your tax returns—and/or if there is a record of default on an installment agreement in the past, the IRS will not establish an installment agreement until you are compliant.

As we discussed in Chapter 6, the general rule is that an OIC is not available to taxpayers who can afford to pay their liability by installment. Remember, if your monthly disposable income is sufficient for you to fully pay the amount owed over the remaining time left on the collection statute of limitations plus five years, you will not qualify for an OIC, but you will probably qualify for an installment agreement.

If you have access to other credit sources, you may want to seriously consider borrowing elsewhere to pay your IRS debt instead of arranging an installment agreement. Here's why: When you are paying on an installment agreement, the IRS—like most creditors who offer revolving credit arrangements—will assess interest and, if applicable, penalties on the unpaid balance of your tax debt. IRS interest rates are subject to change quarterly and may increase, which means your payment could go up. If you miss a payment, you could be subject to an additional failure to pay penalty of up to 1 percent each month. On top of this is the user fee the IRS charges to set up the agreement, which is $52 for agreements where payments are deducted directly from your bank account or $105 if you'd rather write a check each month. Certain low-income taxpayers may qualify for a reduced user fee of $43. The IRS will normally file a Notice of Federal Tax Lien against your property to secure the government's interest against other creditors while the installment agreement is in effect. This could seriously hinder your ability to obtain credit for other reasons during the time you are paying off your tax debt. Defaulting on the agreement could prompt the IRS to take aggressive collection action, and the IRS will typically be less agreeable to negotiating with you if you are unable to make your installment payments as originally agreed than other creditors might be.

You may find that the interest, fees, and other terms associated with a traditional loan or credit card may be more advantageous than what is offered by the IRS—and would not include the federal tax

Installment Agreements

lien. If you have assets you have been trying to avoid liquidating, you may want to reconsider that when you see the total picture of an IRS installment agreement.

> **RESPECTFULLY QUOTED**
>
> "I wish the government would put a tax on pianos for the incompetent."
> —Dame Edith Sitwell

Having said all this, it may be that an IRS installment agreement is your best—or perhaps your only—option. There are several types of installment agreements. Let's take a look at them so you can decide which one would work best for your situation.

Guaranteed Agreement

This agreement is available to individual taxpayers (not businesses) who owe less than $10,000, are not able to presently pay the liability in full, and have not had an IA under this provision within the last five years. You must be able to satisfy the liability in three years. Generally no financial statement is required, although the IRS may request one. This agreement applies to income tax or unpaid out of business employment taxes only.

Streamlined Agreement

This type of IA is available to taxpayers who owe less than $25,000 and are not able to pay the full amount owed at present. You must agree to completely satisfy the liability and keep all other taxes current over the five-year term of the agreement. As with the guaranteed agreement, financial information is usually not required and the agreement applies to income tax or out of business employment taxes only.

High Dollar Agreement

This agreement is designed for taxpayers who owe more than $25,000 and are unable to pay the liability in full at present. The IRS understands that you may need more time than is allowed under the guaranteed or streamlined agreement programs. Under the high dollar plan, you must agree to fully satisfy your liability prior to the expiration of the statue of limitations or agree to a one-time extension of the statute of limitations for up to five additional years, as well as to keep all taxes current in the interim. High dollar installment agreements require a full and complete financial disclosure. If the taxpayer is a corporation, the IRS will require complete financial disclosures from all officers and some employees of the company.

The high dollar agreement allows for some flexibility with your monthly payments. Let's say that you intend to adjust your lifestyle to increase your monthly disposable income but it's going to take a while for you to do it—for example, if you rent and plan to move to a less expensive apartment when your current lease expires—you can propose a payment of a certain amount for a period of time and then have the payment increase.

> **TAX FACT**
> The most common—and biggest—mistake people make when dealing with the IRS is to do nothing.

Partial Payment Agreement

This is essentially a hybrid of an offer in compromise and an installment agreement. Under this plan, the IRS agrees to accept installment payments that will result in a partial payment of the tax liability. To qualify for a Partial Payment Installment Agreement (PPIA), you must provide complete financial information that will be reviewed and verified. You'll also be required to address equity in assets that can be utilized to reduce the outstanding liability.

If you are granted a PPIA, you will be subject to a financial review every two years for the duration of the agreement. If your financial condition has improved, the amount of your payments could increase or the agreement could be terminated. If your financial condition has deteriorated, the amount of your payments could be decreased.

Apply for a PPIA using Form 9465 Request for Installment Agreement. Along with the completed form, you should submit a letter detailing why you are requesting lower payments and full financial disclosure (433-A and/or 433-B) with documentation.

Setting Up an Installment Agreement

To set up an installment agreement if you owe less than $25,000 in combined tax, penalties, and interest, you can use the web-based online payment agreement application at www.irs.gov. If you don't want to do this online, or if you owe more than $25,000, you'll need to complete Form 9465 Installment Agreement Request. If you owe more than $25,000, you'll also need to complete a Form 433-F Collection Information Statement.

HIGHLIGHTS

- If you can't afford to pay your taxes in a lump sum and you don't qualify for an offer in compromise, you should be able to set up an installment agreement to pay the debt off over time.
- You may find that it's more advantageous to obtain a traditional loan or use a credit card to pay your taxes over time than it is to set up an installment agreement with the IRS.
- The basic types of installment agreements the IRS uses are a guaranteed agreement; a streamlined agreement; a high dollar agreement; and a partial payment agreement.
- You can apply for an installment agreement online at www.irs.gov or by using Form 9465 Installment Agreement Request.

8

Communicating with the IRS

Nobody communicates with the IRS or any other taxing authority just for fun. When you make a call or write a letter to the IRS, chances are it involves either a substantial amount of money or the potential for serious consequences. With that in mind, you should use proportionate care when communicating with the IRS. This is not a casual phone call, nor is it an e-mail to a friend about what you're going to do this weekend where a mistake doesn't really matter; this is a conversation with or a letter to the federal government about a tax issue where a mistake could cost you a lot of money.

Whenever possible, your communication with the IRS should be in writing so that you have a record of exactly what was discussed and what the next actions on either your part or the part of the IRS should be. If you talk to an IRS representative either on the phone or in person, make notes of whom you spoke with and the details of the conversation, then follow up with a letter confirming your understanding of what happened. Send all correspondence to the IRS by a trackable method, such as certified mail or a courier service such as FedEx or UPS. If you send a fax, keep the transmission report from the fax machine.

If you are submitting an offer in compromise, you will be required to write an explanation of your circumstances and the reasons you believe you qualify to have your offer accepted. In fact, for most resolutions, it's advisable to send a clearly-written letter along with the request documenting your circumstances and attempts to resolve the situation. This isn't a conversation where an interviewer can ask you questions and you can confirm that you have been understood. This is a one-way transfer of information and it needs to be right the first time.

All correspondence regarding your case must be clear, easy to understand, and include all pertinent facts without rambling. Creativity and cuteness will not earn you any points with the IRS. Clarity and brevity are what count. Explain your position in a way that leaves no questions unanswered. At the same time, you must avoid providing so much extraneous information that your letter is confusing and difficult to follow. Write everything the IRS needs to know and then stop.

It's best to begin with an outline. Use the worksheet on page 89 to help you remember and organize the critical facts that must be in your letter. The worksheet will also help you determine which facts should be included and what should be left out. The IRS' review will be centered on specifics that can be documented, not opinions or feelings. Using a cover letter to tell the IRS what the documents you are sending mean and why you have included particular documents is a good way to start.

When the first draft of your letter has been written, put it aside for a few hours. Give it—and yourself—a rest. It's always

TAX FACT

A soft notice is a statement issued by the IRS on Form CP 2057 to let taxpayers know they should check their tax returns for mistakes. The soft notice does not *require* any action, but if you address the notice, review the return, and correct any errors by filing an amended tax return, you may save yourself a lot of trouble and possibly even additional tax debt in the future.

> **HOW TO USE THE IRS LETTER WORKSHEET TO WRITE YOUR LETTER**
>
> 1. Begin the first paragraph by stating the purpose of your letter using the request summary from your worksheet. Your letter should begin something like this: "I am submitting an offer in compromise [type of OIC] because [what you summarized as the primary reasons on your worksheet]."
> 2. The second paragraph should state the facts and circumstances in the order they occurred. You can open this paragraph with something like: "The following is a list of pertinent facts as they occurred." Then list each separate point in bullet point format. Most people find this way of communicating complex information easier than trying to put the same data in narrative form.
> 3. With each major point, think of any documentation you might include to prove the statement; assign a number to it; and make a reference to it in your letter. Example: "My laptop computer with my financial records was stolen on July 25, 2009 (see police report attachment #2)."
>
> Conclude your letter with a brief summary of no more than two to four sentences.

easier to proofread and revise something that you haven't looked at for a while. When you have corrected and revised your letter to the point that you think it's perfect, ask a friend or relative to read it, then ask them questions to make sure they understood your position. If they can follow your letter and explain what you are asking, you have done a good job. If they can't, revise the letter until it's clear and complete.

Supporting documentation that substantiates your request is also important. For instance, if your special circumstances are health-related, you should attach medical affidavits or a physician's statement. Copies of hospital or doctor bills might also help to prove your case. Identify each attachment by both title and a number so that you can refer to it in your letter. For example: "My hospital bill indicates that I was discharged on Sept. 2, 2010 (see attachment #6)."

Do *not* send original documents to the IRS—ever! Always send the IRS copies. If the IRS needs to see an original document, you can work with the agent handling your case to make it available for inspection.

When your letter and all the supporting documentation is complete and ready to send, make a copy of the entire package so you have an exact duplicate of what you sent, down to the documents in the same order.

HIGHLIGHTS

- Keep records of every contact you have with the IRS in a well-organized log.
- Send all correspondence to the IRS using a trackable method such as certified mail.
- Never send original documents to the IRS.
- Make a complete copy of every information package you send to the IRS.

Communicating with the IRS

IRS LETTER WORKSHEET

Summarize your request and the primary reason(s) for it in one sentence:

_____

_____

_____

List each relevant fact about your case:

a._____

b._____

c._____

d._____

e._____

f._____

g._____

h._____

i._____

j._____

k._____

l._____

When you have finished listing the facts and events relative to your case, go back and number each in the order it occurred. At the same time, delete any facts that are not absolutely necessary to effectively communicating your story.

Sample Letters

On the following pages are sample letters you may use as a guide for composing your own letter to the IRS. Keep in mind that these are only examples and they may not apply to your particular situation, so do not copy them verbatim. See the table at the end of chapter for a way to record IRS communications.

Sample letter detailing special circumstances in support of an OIC submitted on the basis of effective tax administration

January 21, 2011

Internal Revenue Service
Memphis, TN 37501

Re: Offer in Compromise—Effective Tax Administration

Taxpayer: John S. Smith
SSN: 123-45-6789
Address: 321 Main St.
            Anytown, State 12345

Tax Period: 2009

I am submitting an Offer in Compromise—Effective Tax Administration because to obtain the cash necessary to pay my tax obligation would cause an extreme hardship.

I am 71 years old and my wife is 68. We are retired and our only source of income is Social Security. I have terminal cancer and, according to my doctor (see physician's statement attachment #1), I am not expected to live longer than two more years. My wife has congestive heart failure (see physician's statement attachment #2) and is unable to work. Although we have about $80,000 in equity in our home, which is worth about $120,000 (see property appraiser's record attachment #3), I cannot borrow against the equity because it is obvious, from my income, that I would not be able to repay the loan.

I respectfully request that you accept my offer in order to extend to my wife and myself the opportunity to live in a relatively comfortable condition for the remaining short time I have left.

Sincerely,

John S. Smith

Sample letter detailing special circumstances in support of an OIC submitted on the basis of effective tax administration

January 21, 2011

Internal Revenue Service
Memphis, TN 37501

Re: Offer in Compromise—Effective Tax Administration

Taxpayer: John S. Smith
SSN: 123-45-6789
Address: 321 Main St.
               Anytown, State 12345

Tax Period: 2009

I am submitting an Offer in Compromise—Effective Tax Administration because to obtain the cash necessary to pay my tax obligation in full would cause an extreme hardship.

I was rendered unable to work because of an accident two years ago (see medical statement attachment #1). I am currently drawing Social Security disability benefits. That amount is insufficient to pay the necessary expenses of my home in addition to taking care of my wife and two minor children who are still in public schools. While I was in an optimum earning condition, I was able to accumulate some money in IRAs and other savings plans in the approximate amount of $90,000 (see financial statement attachment #2).

I am offering $10,000 to you in settlement of my delinquent taxes and respectfully request that you accept my offer as being in the best interest of the government and myself. I have previously met all my tax responsibilities but I am now unable to pay what I owe without depriving myself and my family of the fundamental day-to-day needs of a four-member family.

Sincerely,

John S. Smith

Sample letter providing documentation in support of an OIC submitted on the basis of doubt as to liability

January 21, 2011

Internal Revenue Service
Memphis, TN 37501

Re: Offer in Compromise—Doubt as to Liability

Taxpayer: John S. Smith
SSN: 123-45-6789
Address: 321 Main St.
            Anytown, State 12345
Tax Period: 2009

I am submitting an Offer in Compromise—Doubt as to Liability because I do not believe I owe the tax in your notice dated December 19, 2010.

When my returns were examined in 2010, I was unable to produce the documentation for my advertising expenses and rental payments for my business. Since that time, I have located the documents to support my deductions for these items and that proof is attached (see advertising receipts attachments #1, 2, and 3 and rental statement attachment #4). I am submitting copies of the original documents, which I have retained. If you require the originals, please let me know.

Please review the attached information and update my file accordingly.

Sincerely,

John S. Smith

Sample letter requesting an abatement of penalties

January 21, 2011

Internal Revenue Service
Memphis, TN 37501

Re: Abatement of Penalties

Taxpayer: John S. Smith, Mary T. Smith
SSN: 123-45-6789
Address: 321 Main St.
Anytown, State 12345

Tax Period: 2008

We have received a penalty notice from your office and wish to resolve this problem. Apparently we received income of which we were unaware from the Dockworkers' Credit Union in 2008.

We do not dispute that we owe the tax, and we do sincerely apologize for this oversight. However, please consider abating the penalty assessed to this tax liability due to the following reasons:

1. We have been very good taxpayers of record and have never had a problem with the IRS before.

2. We did not receive the necessary forms from the Dockworkers' Credit Union to include on our return and were not aware of this income until we received the IRS notification.

3. The amount overlooked was very small.

4. We are both in our 80s, live on a fixed income, and are in poor health. Paying this penalty on top of the tax would cause us financial problems.

I have included statement from our doctors (see attachments #1 and 2) and some financial information (see attachments #3 and 4) to prove the statements above.

Thank you for your consideration in this matter.

Sincerely,

John S. and Mary T. Smith

Sample letter requesting an abatement of penalties

January 21, 2011

Internal Revenue Service
Memphis, TN 37501

Re: Abatement of Penalties

Taxpayer: John S. Smith
SSN: 123-45-6789
Address: 321 Main St.
              Anytown, State 12345
Tax Period: 2007

I wish to request an abatement of penalty assigned to me. I have researched the reasons for which the IRS will consider abating a penalty and believe my situation fits your parameters.

On March 15, 2007, I called the IRS office in my city and spoke to Mary Brown. She told me I could claim my nephew as an exemption because he stays at my house for four months every year. I have since found out that is not correct. This incorrect information caused me to pay the wrong amount of tax.

I understand I owe the taxes and am willing to pay them. However, I don't think I should be penalized because I was advised to do the wrong thing. I have attached a copy of the records I kept detailing my contacts with the IRS (see IRS Communication Log attachment #1). You can see Mary Brown's ID number is 12345.

I have always paid my taxes on time and have never been assessed a penalty before. Please consider my request.

Sincerely,

John S. Smith

IRS COMMUNICATION RECORD

Date, Method of Contact	IRS Representative	Communication	Action List
Date _____ ___ Mail ___ Phone ___ E-Mail	Name _____ Title _____ Address _____ Phone _____ E-Mail _____ ID# _____	Subject: Outcome:	Item: Deadline:
Date _____ ___ Mail ___ Phone ___ E-Mail	Name _____ Title _____ Address _____ Phone _____ E-Mail _____ ID# _____	Subject: Outcome:	Item: Deadline:
Date _____ ___ Mail ___ Phone ___ E-Mail	Name _____ Title _____ Address _____ Phone _____ E-Mail _____ ID# _____	Subject: Outcome:	Item: Deadline:

9

When You Fail to Pay Your Payroll Taxes

One of the more common ways small business owners get into trouble with the IRS is by getting behind on their payroll taxes. Normally you would pay your employees, withhold the appropriate taxes (income and employment taxes), and remit those funds along with your (as the employer) share of your federal tax deposit to the IRS on a monthly or quarterly schedule (depending on the size of your payroll). When you pay your employees, withhold the appropriate taxes, and then don't send the funds to the IRS, you can find yourself in serious trouble.

When cash is tight, you may be tempted to "borrow" from your payroll taxes to fund your operating expenses. Don't do it! Using payroll taxes as a source of working capital can result in a range of problems that can be very expensive to resolve. The interest and penalties (as much as 100 percent) the IRS charges for late payroll tax filing and payment is exorbitant, making that money a very high-priced "short-term loan." The interest and penalties mount quickly, creating a financial burden you may not be able to overcome. And if the business can't pay the tax debt, certain individuals can be held personally liable.

That money does not belong to your company; it belongs to your employees from the time you issue your payroll and must be sent to the IRS on schedule. Using payroll tax money for any other reason is illegal. To guard against temptation, budget the gross pay for your employees plus your portion of the Social Security and Medicare taxes, and make sure you have those funds available when you need them.

The Trust Fund Recovery Penalty

If you're already in the challenging situation of having used payroll tax funds for other purposes, we're going to discuss what you can do about it, but first let me explain the law and how it works.

Congress passed a law that provides for the Trust Fund Recovery Penalty (TFRP) to encourage the prompt payment of withheld income and employment taxes. These taxes are called trust fund taxes because you're holding money in your account that actually belongs to your employees until you make a federal tax deposit in that amount. So in simple language, if you use that money for any reason other than to make the appropriate tax payment, you are stealing from your employees—and the IRS takes a very dim view of that. And if the IRS can't collect delinquent payroll taxes from your company, it will come after you individually.

According to the IRS, the TFRP may be assessed against any person who is responsible for collecting or paying withheld income and employment taxes or for paying collected excise taxes and willfully fails to collect or pay them. A responsible person is defined as a person or group of people who has the duty to perform and the power to direct the collecting, accounting, and paying of trust fund taxes. This could include officers, owners, partners, directors, shareholders, employees (even employees who are not owners), or anyone

Whe You Fail to Pay Your Payroll Taxes

with authority and control over funds to direct their reimbursement. An employee is not a responsible person if his function was solely to pay the bills as directed by a superior and did not actually determine which creditors would and would not be paid. But it's important for you to understand (and I realize I maybe be getting redundant on this point) that if you are a responsible person under the TFRP definition, you may be held personally responsible for all or a portion of the company's tax debt) you are not protected by the company if the company can't pay.

It's also important that you know this: The IRS' goal is to collect the taxes your business owes, and it doesn't care what sort of damage might be done to your company in the process. The IRS can padlock your doors, seize your equipment, and even contact your customers to intercept future payments owed to you.

> **TAX FACT**
> The IRS has about 93,000 to 99,000 (exact figures were unavailable) employees. They range from attorneys, return processors, officers who enforce tax laws, people who oversee operations, and many other positions.

Don't Wait to Take Action

If you owe back taxes personally, you may be able to successfully resolve your situation with the IRS on your own. If your company owes payroll, employment, or any other taxes that would be subject to the TFRP, I recommend that you seek professional assistance immediately. This is not a relatively innocent tax situation; it's a federal crime. You need to move quickly to protect your business and negotiate the business tax relief you need while keeping your company operating.

Your options for dealing with delinquent employment

> **RESPECTFULLY QUOTED**
> "The heart of IRS abuse lies in the existing tax code. Most of the folks who work for the IRS are good people just trying to do their job, but they are caught in a bad, overextended tax system."
> —J. C. Watts, Jr.

and payroll taxes are essentially the same as they are for back personal taxes: You can pay them in full, negotiate an offer in compromise, or set up an installment agreement. However, while the regulations and resolutions are the same, resolving payroll taxes is much more challenging than resolving a personal tax debt. If your business is still operating, you will probably have to pay at least the amount of the TFRP. You may be granted a temporary delay due to hardship, but the key word there is temporary—this is not a final solution. A qualified professional will help you determine the best course of action and will deal with the IRS on your behalf so that you can focus on your business.

HIGHLIGHTS

- A common way for business owners to get into trouble with the IRS is by getting behind on their payroll taxes.
- Do not "borrow" from your payroll taxes to fund your operating expenses. Using payroll tax money for any other reason is illegal.
- If the IRS cannot collect delinquent payroll taxes from your company, it will come after you individually.
- To collect payroll taxes, the IRS can padlock your doors, seize your equipment, and even contact your customers to intercept future payments owed to you.
- Your options for dealing with delinquent employment and payroll taxes are to pay them in full, negotiate an offer in compromise, or set up an installment agreement.
- If you are behind on your payroll taxes, seek assistance from a qualified professional.

10

IRS Audits: Take Them Seriously, But Don't Panic

Few things are more frightening and intimidating to the American taxpayer than the prospect of an IRS audit. While those feelings are understandable and no one should ever take an audit notice from the IRS lightly, there is also no reason for you to be frightened or intimidated when the IRS decides to take a closer look at your return.

The IRS does not use the term *audit* (which means to examine carefully for accuracy with the intent of verification); it uses the term *examine* (which means to analyze, observe, look over carefully, or inspect). At the risk of sounding like a petulant teenager, my response to that is: *Whatever.* The results are the same.

That your return is being examined does not necessarily mean that the IRS believes you have made an error or have been dishonest. There are times when the audit results in no change to your return or tax owed—and may even result in a refund. If you are notified by the IRS that your return has been selected for examination, the two most important things for you to remember are:

1. Stay calm.
2. Respond appropriately and within the required timeframe.

Panic won't help and action is essential. Like other tax problems, you can't ignore an audit notice and hope it will go away, because it won't. The information in this chapter will take the mystery out of the process for you so you know what to expect and what you need to do.

The basic types of audits are:

- Matching
- Correspondence
- Office
- Field
- Research
- Criminal investigation

I have listed the types of audits in order of complexity. As the audit itself becomes more complex, the level of expertise and rank of the IRS staff person you'll deal with increases as well. It's possible that any one of these audits could escalate to the next level or even jump up several levels. For example, a correspondence audit could be settled with a single response from you to the IRS, or it could get so complicated that it's referred to a tax compliance officer for an office audit. A basic office audit (where you go to the IRS office) could escalate to a field audit (where the IRS comes to you). Criminal investigations usually come from office or field audits or a referral from another law enforcement agency.

When you go into a face-to-face audit, always assume that you are right and never ask what you did wrong. Relax and focus on the issues raised by the examiner. And remember that no matter how the audit turns out, you have the right to appeal. Also, the agent handling your audit cannot lien, levy, seize your assets, or send you to jail. All he does is examine your return and put his findings into a report.

> **DO YOU NEED REPRESENTATION?**
>
> Whether or not you need representation when responding to an audit notice is a decision you have to make. In general, most taxpayers can handle a matching audit and even a simple correspondence audit on their own. However, when it comes to office or field audits where you are talking on the phone and meeting face-to-face with an IRS agent, I highly recommend that you retain qualified representation.
>
> Even honest taxpayers can be their own worst enemy during an audit. When you aren't familiar with IRS procedures and you don't know for sure what the agent is trying to find out, it's easy to say the wrong thing and complicate the issue. You can't refuse to speak with the IRS; it has the right to talk with the taxpayer. But you can insist on having a representative with you either in person or via phone conference to guide you through the process—and in my opinion, you would be foolish not to.

Let's take a look at each type of audit so you can understand their purposes, how they are handled by the IRS, and what you should expect if your return is examined.

Type of Audit—Matching

The IRS matches the information on tax returns to the information provided by payors. If an entity reports having paid you money that does not show up on your return, you'll receive a letter about it from the IRS. The letter will likely be several pages long and it's important that you read it completely and carefully. The letter will also clearly state the timeframe during which you must respond. The IRS typically gives you 30 days, but you should always look for the deadline and be sure you respond before that date. If you fail to respond, you'll get another letter called a Statutory Notice of Deficiency which states that you owe whatever amount was indicated in the first letter and allows you 90 days to petition the tax court if you disagree. About two weeks after that 90-day period ends, you'll get a bill and you can expect the IRS to enforce collection.

In the initial letter, following the explanation of what the IRS found that didn't match your return, there will be a place for you to agree or disagree. Let's say the IRS finds a W-2 or 1099 with income you forgot to include on your return, perhaps because you moved or for some other reason didn't receive the document and you overlooked it when preparing your return. There's no dispute about the accuracy of the IRS' position, so all you need to do is mark the box that says you agree, return the form with your check for the additional tax due, and the case is closed. If you don't agree, indicate that in the appropriate place, and return the form with your explanation and supporting documentation.

The irony is that if you report income that does not have a corresponding payor in the IRS files, the agency will simply accept your word for it that you received the money. But if someone else reports having paid you money and you don't include that information on your tax return because you did not actually receive the money, or the amount reported on your tax return is less than what the payor reports, the IRS expects *you* to contact the payor to have the correct amount reported or pay the appropriate tax.

> **RESPECTFULLY QUOTED**
>
> "Worried about an IRS audit? Avoid what's called a red flag. That's something the IRS always looks for. For example, say you have some money left in your bank account after paying taxes. That's a red flag."
>
> —Jay Leno

Type of Audit—Correspondence

From a procedure perspective, a correspondence audit is similar to a matching audit. In a correspondence audit, the IRS sees an item on your return that it wants to question. The issue doesn't require a face-to-face meeting, but instead can be easily handled through letters.

Typically a correspondence audit deals with just one item, often by asking you to send in supporting documentation. For example, if there's a question about your charitable contributions, the IRS could send a letter asking to see the documents supporting the specific

IRS Audits

deductions. You should respond by submitting copies (never originals) of the appropriate documents, such as receipts or statements from the charities. If the IRS accepts your documentation, you'll get a letter acknowledging that. If not, you'll get what's known as an audit report stating that the deduction has been disallowed

> **TAX FACT**
>
> The IRS tries to audit tax returns as soon as possible after they are filed. Most audits will be of returns filed within the last two years; however, the IRS can include returns filed within the last three years and, if a substantial error is identified, go back further but generally not more than the last six years.

and giving you the balance due. You'll be given time to respond to that, but if you don't, a Statutory Notice of Deficiency will be issued. You will be allowed 90 days to petition the tax court before the tax is officially assessed and enforced collection begins.

Type of Audit—Office

In an office audit, you will be advised that your return for a specific year is being examined and that the IRS would like you to come into its office and bring documents supporting certain claims. The individual who conducts an office audit is a tax compliance officer; you'll often see "TCO" next to their signature.

Office audits typically cover three or four items (as compared to just one issue in a correspondence audit) and are likely going to require some discussion. You can expect to spend anywhere from two hours to a half day reviewing the information with the tax compliance officer. At the end of the meeting, if there will be no change in your tax liability (and yes, that really does happen), the IRS will issue what is called a "No Change" letter for your records. If there will be a change, the TCO may give you a final audit report with a balance due or a decrease in tax liability. If you were unable to completely address every item during your meeting, instead of issuing a final audit report, the TCO may schedule another appointment.

Once the TCO gives you the audit report with his decision, you have 30 days to respond or pay. If you respond and the result is a revised report, you'll have 10 to 15 days to respond to that—you won't get another 30 days. This is why it's critical that you read everything the IRS sends or gives you and pay attention to the deadlines. If you disagree with the audit report and the tax is less than $25,000, you can appeal by simply writing a statement explaining your position. If the tax is more than $25,000, you'll need to file a formal protest. Refer to IRS Publication 5 and Publication 556 (available at www.irs.gov) for instructions on how to do this.

TAX FACT

When your return is being audited, the IRS will provide you with a written request for the documents needed. The IRS will accept some electronic records; contact your auditor to determine what can be accepted. If the auditor asks you for any information beyond what was in the original written request, insist that the revised request be made in writing according to IRS protocol.

If you don't respond by the deadline, a Statutory Notice of Deficiency will be issued, giving you 90 days to petition the tax court if you disagree. If you fail to do that, the tax will be assessed.

Normally, the TCO will not issue more than two audit reports. If you don't agree with the second one, the next step is to request an appeals conference. When you do that, your case is sent to the appeals division, which is completely separate from the examination division. The statutory notice is put on hold until the appeals division makes a ruling. That can take up to a year, but the IRS cannot assess tax unless a statutory notice is issued. However, interest will continue to accrue during this period.

Type of Audit—Field

A field examination is similar to an office exam, except a revenue agent comes to your premises instead of you going to the IRS office. While there are some exceptions, typically field examinations are conducted on businesses, and you won't have a revenue agent come to your home unless you're operating a homebased business. Of course, there may be exceptions to this, depending on your particular situation. However, revenue agents have a higher level of expertise and are paid more than the people who handle correspondence and office audits, so the IRS doesn't like to tie them up with small examinations that aren't likely to generate much in the way of additional tax. When they come out, they're going to want to look at all your books and records and compare that information to what's on your tax return. You can expect a field examination to take a minimum of two to three days, and often a lot longer than that.

It's not always convenient, especially for small and homebased operations, to have a revenue agent set up in your location for several days or longer, as is the case in large audits. If your facility can't accommodate a revenue agent working there for several days, you can request that the agent make other arrangements. For example, we had a client who ran a homebased employee benefits company and didn't have a place in her home where the agent could comfortably work without disrupting her operation. The agent still wanted to see where the business was conducted, but we were able to successfully limit the time the agent spent in her home.

In another case, our client had a homebased business that was no longer operating. She was still living in the home and her elderly mother who was in poor health lived with her. Our client felt that having the agent in her home would be too stressful for her mother. We were able to convince the agent that since the business no longer existed, there was no purpose to an on-site visit. We've had countless other clients over the years who run small retail stores; having an IRS agent on the premises for several days would intimidate their customers and harm their business, and we have been successful in limiting the amount of time the agent spends on site.

With that said, it's important to understand that in a field audit of a return for an ongoing business, the agent is going to need to at least see your facility, even if he doesn't complete the entire audit there. If you want to object to having the revenue agent working on your premises, you need to have a valid reason. And if you think having a revenue agent on site for several days is inconvenient, imagine what it's like at large corporations—the agents pretty much move in and can spend as much as a year completing the audit.

TAX FACT

If it's time for your appointment with the IRS auditor and you don't have all the information requested, contact the auditor at the telephone number listed in the notification letter. The auditor may decide to begin the audit with what you have rather than postponing the appointment. If the initial appointment is scheduled beyond 45 days from the initial action, managerial approval is required.

You don't have to allow the IRS to enter your private property, such as the private living area of your home (assuming you have a homebased business) or even the private areas of your business that are not open to the public, unless the agent has a search warrant, which doesn't happen in the case of a routine audit. If an agent wants to come to your home and it is not your place of business (or was not your place of business during the relative tax period), you can politely respond that you would prefer to meet in the agent's office. If an agent is at your place of business and expresses a desire to see a private area, you are within your rights to explain that you will bring whatever information the agent needs to the public area where the agent is working.

Type of Audit—Research

These are the audits that everyone dreads: the examinations that verify every line item on your return. The IRS conducts these audits to gather information so it can identify the areas it needs to focus on for compliance in future years. The revenue agent will not only look at every detail of your tax return, she'll also examine your bank records and other documents. The returns chosen for this audit are selected at random to get a statistical sampling—it doesn't mean that your return has raised any questions. Of course, if the revenue agent finds any errors or claims you can't substantiate, it will be handled appropriately.

It will likely come as little comfort to you, but the revenue agents who conduct these audits dread doing them probably almost as much as the taxpayer dreads having to go through them.

> **TAX FACT**
> When you meet with an IRS representative for an office or field examination, you will be given a copy of the Privacy Act Statement and a brochure that explains what your appeals rights are. You always have the right to appeal the result of an audit.

Type of Audit—Criminal Investigation

This is not actually part of the regular audit process; it happens when other circumstances cause the IRS to take another look at your returns. Sometimes a criminal investigation begins when, during a routine audit, a tax compliance officer or revenue agent finds indicators of criminal activity and refers the case to the Criminal Investigation Division. Or it might be that a law enforcement agency makes an arrest for crimes that generate income (such as embezzlement, prostitution, illegal drug sales, theft, and so on) and sends a referral to the IRS so the government can determine if the income was reported and taxed, and, if not, how much tax is owed.

The IRS staffers who work in this unit are called special agents. If anyone ever comes to your home or office and identifies himself as a special agent with the IRS, you need to call a

> **TAX FACT**
> It's possible that your tax return may be audited simply because of the tax preparer you used. If the IRS identifies a particular preparer as being routinely negligent or even fraudulent, it may cause them to look at every return that individual has prepared, and you may or may not be told that this is the reason you are being audited.

SEVEN IMPORTANT FACTS ABOUT YOUR APPEAL RIGHTS

The IRS provides an appeals system for those who do not agree with the results of a tax return examination or with other adjustments to their tax liability. Here are the top seven things you should know when it comes to your appeal rights.

1. When the IRS makes an adjustment to your tax return, you will receive a report or letter explaining the proposed adjustments. This letter will also explain how to request a conference with an Appeals office should you not agree with the IRS findings on your tax return.

2. In addition to tax return examinations, many other tax obligations can be appealed. You may also appeal penalties, interest, trust fund recovery penalties, offers in compromise, liens, and levies. However, it's important to understand that interest is statutory and accrues with any unpaid balance. Generally the IRS will only mitigate interest when the agency has made a mistake that has caused the harm of additional interest charges.

3. You are urged to be prepared with appropriate records and documentation to support your position if you request a conference with an IRS Appeals employee.

4. Although appeals conferences are informal meetings and you can represent yourself, you have the right to representation. Those allowed to represent taxpayers include attorneys, certified public accountants, or enrolled agents (individuals who have been enrolled to practice before the IRS). See IRS Publication 1, "Your Rights as a Taxpayer" for more information about representation.

5. The IRS Appeals Office is separate from—and independent of—the IRS office taking the action you may disagree with. The Appeals Office is the only level of administrative appeal within the agency.

6. If you do not reach agreement with IRS Appeals or if you do not wish to appeal within the IRS, you may appeal certain actions through the courts.

7. For further information on the appeals process, refer to Publication 5, "Your Appeal Rights and How to Prepare a Protest

> If You Don't Agree." This publication, along with more on IRS appeals is available at www.irs.gov.
>
> *Source: Internal Revenue Service*

criminal defense attorney immediately.

How Does the IRS Select Returns for Examination?

The IRS uses a variety of methods to select returns for examination.

The agency actively works to identify promoters and participants of fraudulent tax avoidance transactions, such as the ones mentioned in Chapter 2. If the IRS receives information indicating you may be a participant in such a transaction, your returns will likely be examined.

The IRS also uses a computer scoring system based on the information gathered from the research audits. The Discriminant Function System (DIF) score rates the potential for change and the Unreported Income DIF (UIDIF) score rates the return for the potential of unreported income. The formulas used to calculate these scores are kept confidential—even people inside the IRS don't know exactly what they are. When you have an item on your return that's outside the norm, it's flagged by the computer and a person takes a look at it and determines if it needs to be examined further.

A classic example is a return that shows very little income and a lot of interest and expense deductions. The IRS is going to want to know what that person is living on and the return will be stamped for examination. The return could be totally legitimate—perhaps a person who recently lost a high-paying job is living off savings or has moved in with a family member, so he has virtually no day-to-day living expenses and is trying to meet his obligations from when he had a higher income. Or it could be that the person is in a cash business and is trying to avoid paying taxes by not reporting all his income—in that case, the IRS is going to attempt to uncover the truth and take appropriate action.

> **TAX FACT**
>
> An audit can be concluded in three ways:
> - No change: You substantiate all of the items being reviewed and there is no change to the tax return.
> - Agree: The IRS proposes changes you understand and with which you agree.
> - Disagree: The IRS proposes changes you understand but with which you do not agree.

Or a taxpayer might take charitable deductions that are higher than the norm. Someone at the IRS will review the entire return and decide if the charitable deductions look reasonable in the overall context of the return. If so, the taxpayer will never know his return was reviewed. If not, he'll likely get a letter asking him to document the charitable contributions.

Returns may be selected for audit when they involve issues or transactions with other taxpayers, such as business partners or investors, whose returns were selected for examination. And some returns are identified for examination in connection with local compliance initiatives, specific market segments, or return preparers. Finally, some returns are selected for audit based on reports of suspected fraud. These reports are often made by former spouses, disgruntled employees, or someone you've ticked off for some reason.

How Are You Notified That You Are Being Audited?

You will always be notified of an audit in writing by regular U.S. mail. It's possible that a revenue agent will give you a call ahead of time to set up the date of the examination, but that call will always be followed up with a letter. During the call the agent will not ask you for any information about your tax return or discuss anything other than setting up a mutually convenient time for a meeting. The tax compliance officer or revenue agent will probably say something like, "Hello, my name is John Smith with the Internal Revenue Service, and I've got your 2008 return for examination. I need to set an appointment with you and I will be following up this call with a confirmation letter. Can we schedule a date and time?" Once you agree on a date, time, and place, you'll be off the phone. The agent will verify your mailing address, but will not ask you any other questions.

You will never receive an audit notification by e-mail. The IRS never initiates any communication via e-mail. Once you have established a working relationship with an IRS agent, you may have some e-mail communications, but any unexpected e-mail you receive that appears to be from the IRS and is not coming from an individual with whom you have had previous mail, telephone, or in-person contact is not legitimate and is likely an attempt to defraud you in some way.

Always respond to an audit notification by the deadline, even if you need additional time to gather the information requested. If you fail to respond to a correspondence audit, you will be assessed the tax on the item in question. If you fail to respond to an office or field examination, you risk the agent doing something known as stripping the return, which means all your expense deductions are removed from the return and you are assessed the tax on that basis.

> **TAX FACT**
> You have the right to record all meetings with the IRS as long as you give notice that you intend to do so with sufficient time to allow the IRS to record also.

HIGHLIGHTS

- The IRS doesn't use the term audit; when a tax return is selected for a review, the IRS calls it an examination.
- The fact that your return has been selected for examination does not necessarily mean that the IRS suspects there is something wrong with your return.
- The basic types of audits are: matching, correspondence, office, field, research, and criminal investigation.
- In a matching audit, the IRS matches information on tax returns to information provided by payors.

- A correspondence audit typically deals with one issue and is something that can be handled by an exchange of letters.
- For an office audit, you will be invited to come to the IRS office to discuss several issues on your tax return.
- A field audit is conducted on your premises and is usually restricted to businesses.
- A research audit is a detailed, line-by-line examination conducted to develop statistical data.
- A criminal investigation is not really an audit, but occurs when something happens to cause the IRS to suspect criminal activity.
- The results of an examination may be no change, an increase in tax liability, or a decrease in tax liability.
- The IRS uses a variety of methods to select returns for examination. A computerized scoring system rates returns for the potential for change. Some returns are selected because they involve transactions related to others that were selected for examination. Sometimes returns are examined because of a report of suspected fraud.
- You will always be notified by mail that you are being audited. If the examination is a field or office audit, you may receive a telephone call setting up an appointment and then a letter confirming it. The IRS never sends out audit notifications by e-mail.

11

Other Taxing Authorities

If you owe back taxes to the federal government, there's an excellent chance you also owe money to some other taxing authority, such as your state or local government. About half the clients who come to JK Harris & Company owe taxes to more than one entity. It could be state income tax, sales tax, employment-related taxes, or a combination of several state-specific taxes. Whatever it is, you probably already know about it, because most states tend to be more aggressive with their collection efforts than the IRS. States also tend to charge more in interest and penalties than the IRS. That often comes as a surprise, but the reason is logical when you compare the difference between a state's budget and the federal budget: The amount you owe to a state is likely to be more significant to the state than the amount you owe to the IRS is to the federal government. Also, states typically do not have the collection resources the IRS does in terms of liens and levies, so they are likely to harass you sooner and to a greater degree than the IRS.

The first step in dealing with other taxing authorities—much like it is with the IRS—is to be sure that all your state tax returns have been filed. As part of this process, if you're an employee in a state with state income tax, be sure you have received accurate withholding information from your employer and that the information you have matches the information your employer has reported to the state. Beyond that, be aware that dealing with state and local taxing authorities can be quite different than dealing with the IRS.

Once you are in compliance with state regulations regarding filing returns and have determined what you owe in back taxes, the next thing you should do is check to see if your state offers any sort of amnesty program. Under these programs, states will take actions such as forgiving interest and penalties if you pay the tax due by a particular date—something the IRS doesn't do. If your state doesn't have an amnesty program, you still have options.

Most states have programs similar to the IRS' offer in compromise and installment agreements, but the state programs are not going to be exactly the same as the federal counterpart. That means qualifying for an OIC with the IRS doesn't mean you'll automatically qualify for it with your state. By the same token, you may not qualify for an OIC with your federal taxes and yet qualify for it with the state. Also, the state's terms may be different—for example, many states that will accept OICs or installment agreements do so with the requirement that the tax be paid within a much shorter period than the federal government allows.

Remember that, just as the federal government can, states can put liens on your property and levy your bank accounts and wages. States can also ask the IRS to send any refunds you may be due to the state to pay off your state liability. I recommend that you do everything possible to avoid a state lien or levy. It's been the experience of the tax professionals at JK Harris that most states are far more reluctant to release a levy or garnishment before the tax liability is paid in full than the federal government is, even after payment arrangements have been made.

Something else a state can do to delinquent taxpayers is to not renew certain licenses until your tax obligation is settled. For example, as I write this book, we are working with a nurse in Indiana who is at risk of losing her job because the state refuses to renew her nursing license until she resolves her back state tax issues. Delinquent state taxes can put a lot of licenses in jeopardy, including various occupational licenses and even driver's licenses.

If you're a business and owe back sales tax, you are at risk of what's called a cash register levy. That's when the state sends a representative into your business to stand at the cash register and take whatever cash comes in. When you think about the impression that would make on your customers, you'll understand why I am advising you to do everything you can to avoid getting to that point. The states are also more likely to shut down a business for delinquent sales tax than the IRS is for other delinquent taxes.

> **RESPECTFULLY QUOTED**
>
> "I am proud to be paying taxes in the United States. The only thing is, I could be just as proud for half the money."
> —*Arthur Godfrey*

Criminal Liability for Back State Taxes

In general, the risk of criminal prosecution for back state taxes is not as great as it is for federal taxes—but that's typically because if a crime is involved, the IRS will likely come after you before the state does. However, several states have provisions for taxing income from criminal activities just as the federal government does. One example is possession of marijuana and other controlled substances: In a few states, possession above a certain amount is considered distribution and you can be taxed on the state level at the street value of whatever controlled substance you had, and that's over and above any criminal prosecution that may take place for the possession charge itself.

Knowledge Is Your Best Defense

It's extremely important that you find out the requirements and procedures of the states in which you owe taxes. Most states offer free workshops for business owners and managers to teach them what they need to do to stay in compliance. These workshops are held periodically and are a great resource, especially if you're starting your business or if you're in a situation where your tax issues might change—for example, if you go from being a sole proprietor to having employees or if you've been selling wholesale and decide to open a retail store. However, if you know you owe back taxes, don't wait to attend a free workshop to figure out what to do. It's critical that you take immediate action. As is the case with federal back taxes, the longer you wait, the bigger your problem will become. If you are not confident in your own ability to handle the situation, consider getting advice from a qualified professional.

> **TAX FACT**
>
> Your state tax liability is not limited to the state in which you live. If you have a business, you could have state tax liability in every state in which you operate. Even individuals can easily have multiple state tax liability. For example, if you live in one state and work in another, which is common for people in the Northeast, you may have to file a resident return for the state in which you live and a non-resident return for the state in which you work.

Where to Go for State Tax Information

A listing of the departments of revenue with contact information is at the back of this book beginning on page 153.

HIGHLIGHTS

- Most states are more aggressive with their collection efforts than the IRS.

- If you owe your state back taxes, the first step is to get in compliance—get all your returns and forms filed so you know where you stand.
- Find out if your state has an amnesty program or programs such as the offer in compromise or installment agreements.
- Some states will refuse to renew various licenses, including driver's and occupational licenses, for individuals who are delinquent in their taxes.
- Businesses that owe back state and/or local sales tax are at risk of a cash register levy, which is when the state sends a representative into your business to stand at your cash register and take whatever money comes in.
- Many individuals and businesses pay local and state taxes in multiple municipalities and states. Find out the requirements and procedures of every state in which you pay taxes.

12

Go It Alone or Get Help?

It's decision time. Now you understand the process of dealing with back tax issues. What are you going to do?

At this point, you have two choices: You can either do nothing or take action.

If you choose to do nothing, your tax problems will continue to escalate. No one—not even the IRS—can force you to deal with your tax issues. Certainly the IRS can make your life miserable until you do, but it cannot make you sit down and do whatever your particular situation requires. If you have decided to do nothing, put this book down now and go back to doing whatever it was you were doing before you picked it up. Just remember where you put it, because I hope that at some point, you'll change your mind.

If you choose to take action, you have three choices: You can handle your tax problems yourself; you can hire a professional to assist you and represent you before the IRS and other taxing authorities; or you can use an online service to guide you.

Should You Do It Yourself?

Should you handle your back tax problems yourself? I can't answer that question for you. You have to decide if you can deal with the process and its accompanying frustrations. Consider how much you owe and what a professional would charge. You also want to factor in the value of your time—is your time better spent dealing with the IRS or doing something more productive while you pay someone to deal with the IRS on your behalf?

> **RESPECTFULLY QUOTED**
>
> "People who complain about taxes can be divided into two classes: men and women."
>
> —Unknown

In my opinion, the two situations that you should definitely not try to handle yourself are if you own a business that owes back payroll taxes (or are in some other capacity being held responsible for back payroll taxes) or if you are the subject of a criminal investigation. Those are circumstances requiring a level of knowledge and expertise the average taxpayer lacks, and the consequences of not having proper advice and representation could be severe. In most other situations, the decision on retaining a professional tax representation firm comes down to personal choice.

Doing It Yourself

If you want to tackle your back tax problem yourself, get to work now. Go back through this book and put together your action plan. Your steps are:

1. **Get in compliance.** Get all your back tax returns and other IRS reports filed and current so you can figure out exactly where you stand.
2. **Evaluate your financial situation.** If you can afford to pay what you owe, do it—no matter how painful it may be. The government is not going to let you decline to pay your taxes just because you don't want to. If you have the resources to borrow (and repay) money, do that and get your taxes paid. This will get

you out from under the burden of being a target of enforced collection activity and let you begin rebuilding the economic side of your life. If you can't pay the full amount right now and can't borrow, consider the offer in compromise program or an installment agreement.

3. **Remember to deal with state taxes.** Check with the taxing authority in every state in which you owe taxes to find out what your options are.

4. **Once you are in compliance, stay that way.** Think about what happened that created your tax problems and put together a plan and a system to keep it from ever happening again. We'll talk more about that in Chapter 13.

> **RESPECTFULLY QUOTED**
>
> "Taxes are the way the government has of artificially inducing the rainy day everybody has been saving for."
> —*Unknown*

Hiring Someone to Help and Represent You

If your tax problem is bigger, more complicated, or more time-consuming than you want to try to handle on your own, consider retaining a firm to help you. Here's what to consider:

First, understand that hiring a tax representation firm doesn't mean that you won't have to put forth any effort in the process. You're going to have to answer questions and provide documentation. Also, there is nothing a professional representative is going to do for you that you can't do for yourself. Even so, there are benefits to having representation. You'll be able to leave the tedious process of filling out forms, analyzing numbers, and negotiating to your representative who is far more familiar with the ins and outs of dealing with the IRS than you are.

We know from experience that, when negotiating on their own, taxpayers tend to say more to the IRS than is necessary and agree to settlements that they aren't likely to be able to complete. Using a professional to represent you allows you to avoid these pitfalls.

Finally, although there are no guarantees and a lot depends on your particular circumstances, chances are you'll get better results by using a professional than by handling your case yourself. Think about it this way: If you have a pair of scissors, you can cut your own hair. But if you're a trained, experienced hair stylist, you're going to do a better job.

Who Can Represent You Before the IRS?

You can always represent yourself when dealing with the IRS. If you want someone else to represent you that individual must meet the requirements to practice before the IRS, which means to deal with all matters connected with a presentation to the IRS on behalf of a taxpayer, including preparing and filing documents, communicating with the IRS, and representing clients at meetings. Any attorney, certified public accountant (CPA), and enrolled agent who is not currently under suspension or disbarment from practice may practice before the IRS.

In addition, an individual may represent an immediate family member; a regular full-time employee of an employer may represent the employer; and a general partner or a regular full-time employee of a partnership may represent the partnership. There are other less common situations when other individuals are permitted to practice before the IRS, although it's usually with limitations based on the circumstances. For example, a tax preparer who is not otherwise qualified to practice before the IRS may represent a taxpayer but only with respect to the return he prepared and signed and only before revenue agents and customer service representatives, not appeals officers, revenue officers, or counsel.

Just because someone *may* represent you before the IRS doesn't mean they *should*. An attorney may represent you, but if his practice doesn't focus on this type of work, he probably isn't going to be as effective as you need. It's also a mistake to assume that all CPAs are tax experts; they are not. CPAs focus on a variety of areas, and many will practice for a lifetime without ever going before the IRS. By contrast, an enrolled agent is a tax professional who has demonstrated special competence in tax matters and has been granted the authority to practice before the IRS.

Selecting the Right Representation

Choosing someone to represent you before the IRS is a lot like choosing a health care provider When you have a routine cold, a walk-in clinic staffed by nurse practitioners can probably provide the diagnosis and treatment you need. But if you have a brain tumor, you're going to want a specialist with extensive training and experience. You have to decide if your particular tax situation is a head cold or a brain tumor, and then make your choice of representation accordingly.

Using an Online Tax Representation Service

An online tax representation service offers you a middle ground between doing it entirely on your own and hiring someone to represent you. At JK Harris Tax Help Online (www.jkharristaxhelponline.com), for example, we use leading-edge technology combined with the knowledge and experience of our professional tax team to allow you to enter your information into a secure website and promptly receive a detailed analysis of your situation along with recommendations for action. After you review that report, you can decide how much you want to do on your own, how much consulting you need, and how much you want us (or any other tax professional) to handle for you. It's a pay-as-you-go plan and you're in control at all times.

Tips for Choosing a Tax Representation Firm

There are a lot of things to consider when selecting a tax representation firm to help you deal with the IRS. These tips will help you make the choice that's best for you.

- Don't make your selection based on advertising alone. Yes, my company spends millions of dollars every year on advertising, as do a number of other tax representation firms. Our ads are designed to get your attention so that you'll call us and we can review your situation and offer our assessment. Make your decision based on the firm's qualifications—not on the skill and creativity of its advertising agency.

- Avoid companies that claim a specific success rate or guarantee results. Every case is different and the IRS makes the final decision, which determines the results. Just because a tax representation firm settled a $100,000 back tax debt for $5,000 for one client doesn't mean you'll get a similar settlement.

- Be sure the firm has a professional staff qualified to practice before the IRS along with a support team of paraprofessionals. Find out who will be handling your case.

- Do your due diligence but put the information in perspective. Consider the big picture as you research the companies you're considering. For example, if you do an internet search on JK Harris & Company, you will see complaints. Do an internet search on a much smaller company, and you won't see as many complaints. Compare the number of complaints to the number of clients served—our ratio is one of the lowest in the industry. Also, consider the source when reading complaints. Many "consumer websites" don't verify the information posted and do not even check to see who is doing the posting. We know this because we monitor the internet and attempt to contact people who post complaints about us. And I think I can speak on behalf of every tax representation firm when I say we find it frustrating when clients complain about us for actions the IRS took that we had no control over. We would be happy to address your concerns about any negative information you may find about us on the internet or elsewhere.

- Ask how fees are calculated. The fee should be based on how much work the firm is going to have to do—not how much you owe or how much the firm thinks it can reduce your tax obligation. For example, our fee structure is based on a point system and we explain in detail how we calculate fees based on the client's individual situation.

- Look for a firm that charges its fees incrementally rather than asking you to pay everything in advance. This gives you the opportunity to assess the initial results and make a decision about proceeding with the case.
- Avoid any firm advertising they have an inside connection at the IRS. Although many firms hire former IRS employees, these employees don't have an inside connection, nor can they negotiate on your behalf any differently than an enrolled agent, CPA, or attorney.
- Many national tax resolution firms conduct their business over the phone, rather than meeting in person. Owing back taxes is a stressful situation and it's important that you be able, if you choose, to meet face-to-face with a tax representation specialist when reviewing your situation and determining the best options. Companies that don't have someone who can meet with you personally both initially and as your case progresses should be viewed with caution.
- Choose a firm with longevity and experience. The tax resolution industry is a fast-growing one and many firms lack the necessary experience to achieve the best possible outcome for you. Remember: The firm you hire will be representing you before the IRS. You want a firm well-versed in taxes and IRS procedures. The process of negotiating with the IRS can be lengthy, often taking months or more than a year. Make sure you hire someone you trust and will be comfortable working with.

HIGHLIGHTS

- You can either represent yourself before the IRS or hire someone to represent you.
- Get in compliance, which means get all your delinquent tax returns and other IRS reports filed.

- Evaluate your financial situation so you know what you can afford to do.
- Remember to deal with state taxes.
- Consider hiring someone to handle the process for you and represent you before the IRS.
- Choose a tax representation firm with care.

13

Stay in Compliance

Though it might seem now as though you'll never get out of the tax mess you're in, the fact is that there truly is light at the end of the tunnel. The process won't be fun and it won't be quick, but there will come a time when your tax problems are resolved and you are in compliance with all applicable tax laws.

When you reach that point, you need to have a plan in place to stay in compliance and avoid ever getting into this situation again. This chapter is not intended to be a complete guide to compliance, but I do want to highlight some of the more important things you should do.

Be Proactive

You have learned the hard way that the IRS expects you to comply with our tax laws. That means filing your returns and making all your tax payments completely, accurately, and on time. It's easy to let things like this get away from you. Now is the time to set up a system so that you will stay on top of your tax issues from now on.

Of course, even as I write this, I recognize that many of our clients are procrastinators. They put off important things, even when they know the consequences are serious. If it's simply not in your nature to be proactive, consider contracting with a service to do it for you. At JK Harris & Company, we offer compliance services for both our individual and business clients. As much as we want your business, we only want to represent you on back tax issues once—and when that's resolved, we want to help you make sure you never have to go through it again.

> **RESPECTFULLY QUOTED**
> "Taxes are what we pay for civilized society."
> —Oliver Wendell Holmes, Jr.

Keep Good Records

This is basic business: Keep good records. Find a system that works for you and use it. For individuals, this could be as simple as setting up a series of file folders in which to keep your receipts and other tax-related documents. Or you may opt to use any of the off-the-shelf accounting packages—they are reasonably priced and easy to learn. And if you are not a bookkeeper, don't try to do that job—hire someone, whether an employee or a firm, to handle it for you.

One point I do want to stress is this: Part of keeping complete, accurate, and current records is filing the appropriate information with the IRS.

As I'm writing this book, my team is working with a client who paid someone cash and took a $30,000 per year deduction as a business expense over several years. The problem is that he can't prove that he made the payments. Also, he didn't withhold taxes and issue a W-2, nor did he file a 1099 to show the payment being made to an independent contractor. He did get a name and social security number from the independent contractor, but he didn't verify it at the time and it has turned out to be false. The IRS has disallowed the deduction, and the tax and interest on that is going to be high. Remember that the IRS takes the position that if it can't get the tax on the other side (meaning from the entity or individual you paid), it's not going to allow you to deduct it. If you are spending money you intend to deduct, do it in a way that provides you with proof if you ever need it.

By the way, you can verify social security numbers through the Social Security Administration. For more information on how to use the Social Security Number Verification Service (SSNVS), visit www.socialsecurity.gov.

We're Here to Help

My goal has been to give what you need to know to take care of your back tax issues once and for all. If you have any questions, a member of the JK Harris & Company team is available to help. Give us a call at (800) 800-3022.

Terms You Should Know

Abatement: a partial or complete cancellation of taxes, interest, or penalties owed by a taxpayer.

Ability to pay: a concept of tax fairness that states that people with different amounts of wealth or different amounts of income should pay tax at different rates; also, a borrower's capability of meeting his or her current and future debt obligations.

Accounting method: a set of rules used to determine when and how income and expenses are reported.

Accounting period: the annual period that an individual or business uses for keeping records and reporting income and expenses.

Accounts payable: short-term liabilities that represent the amounts owed to vendors and creditors for the purchase of supplies, products, parts, or services that were bought on credit and do not bear interest.

Accounts receivable: short-term assets that represent the amount due for the credit sale of products or services to customers.

Accrual basis: the method of record keeping by which income is recorded when earned and expenses are recorded when incurred.

Active participation: when a taxpayer makes significant rental or business management decisions, such as approving rental terms, repairs, expenditures, and new tenants; taxpayers who use a leasing agent or property manager are still considered active participants if they retain final management rights.

Actual expense method: one of two methods (the other is the standard mileage method) for calculating business automobile expenses where the taxpayer determines the actual business portion of expenses for fuel, maintenance, parking fees, tolls, and loan interest.

Adjusted gross income (AGI): gross income reduced by certain amounts, such as a deductible IRA contribution or student loan interest.

Amended tax return: a tax return filed to change a previously filed return.

Amount due: in relation to a tax liability, the amount of money a taxpayer must pay to the government when the total tax due is greater than the total tax payments that have been made.

Appeal: to call for a review of an IRS decision.

Asset: anything owned by an individual or business (real or personal, tangible or intangible) that has commercial or exchange value.

Audit: to examine carefully for accuracy with the intent of verification (see *examine*).

Automated collection system (ACS): a computerized collection process for the IRS to contact taxpayers by telephone or mail and to locate assets for collection action.

Balance due account: IRS term for a delinquent, unpaid account.

Bankruptcy: the legal process under federal statutes that provides for rehabilitation of a debtor through the discharge of certain debts, or through a debt repayment plan over a period of time.

Basis: the cost of an asset owned by a taxpayer.

Blocked income: when a taxpayer cannot convert foreign currency to U.S. dollars due to local law or local government policy; special tax rules allow taxpayers with blocked income to delay reporting part of their income.

Book value: refers to a business' historical cost of assets less the liabilities.

Burden of proof: a formal legal requirement to provide persuasive information or evidence of the legitimacy of a claim.

Business expense: the current ordinary and necessary operating costs of running a business.

Business Master File (BMF): a file maintained by the IRS that contains all tax data and related information pertaining to individual business income taxpayers intended to reflect a continuously updated and current record of each taxpayer's account.

Capital gain or loss: the difference between the market or book value at purchase, or cost of acquisition, and that realized from the sale or disposition of a capital asset.

Capital stock: the ownership of shares of a corporation authorized by its articles of incorporation, including preferred and common stock.

Cash basis: practice of recording income and expenses only when cash is actually received or paid out (see *accrual basis*).

Centralized Authorization File (CAF): an IRS file that contains all Forms 2848, powers of attorney, and Forms 8821 (Tax Information Authorizations).

Chapter 7: chapter of bankruptcy law that provides for a full liquidation of an entity's non-exempt property to satisfy creditors, and discharges all dischargeable debts.

Chapter 11: chapter of bankruptcy law that provides for partial payment of some debts and the partial discharge of some debts belonging to a business.

Chapter 13: chapter of bankruptcy law that provides for the partial payment of some debts and the partial discharge of some debts for an individual.

Child and dependent care credit: a nonrefundable credit that allows taxpayers to claim a credit for paying someone to care for their qualifying dependents under the age of 13 or spouses or other dependents who are unable to care for themselves.

Collection Division: the organizational arm of the IRS with the mission of collecting delinquent taxes and securing delinquent tax returns from individuals, businesses, corporations, trusts, or any other entity that owes IRS money.

Collection due process (CDP) hearing: a hearing to discuss a Notice of Federal Tax Lien or Notice of Intent to Levy with which you disagree.

Collection information statement (CIS): IRS financial statement required from individuals (Form 433-A) and/or businesses (Form 433-B) who owe IRS taxes and have indicated an inability to pay the liability.

Collection statute of limitations: IRS Section 6503 places a limit on the time in which the IRS may collect a tax.

Community property: the holdings and resources owned in common by a husband and wife.

Compensation: something (such as money) given or received as payment or reparation.

Compliance: conforming or acting in accordance with certain standards; the IRS uses the term compliance to mean that all taxes are paid up to date and all returns currently required to be filed are on file with the IRS.

Corporation: the most common form of business organization; one chartered by a state and given many legal rights as an entity separate from its owners.

Cost of goods sold (COGS): the amount determined by subtracting the value of the ending merchandise inventory from the sum of the beginning merchandise inventory and the net purchases for the fiscal period.

Credit: in terms of taxes, a tax credit is a direct reduction of a taxpayer's liability; credits may be allowed for such purposes as child care expenses, higher education costs, qualifying children, and earned income of low-income taxpayers.

Criminal Investigation Division (CID): the organizational arm of the IRS that has the mission to investigate crimes, i.e., fraudulent tax returns, willful failure to file, willful failure to pay, etc.

Currently non-collectible: (see *Status 53*).

Current taxes: taxes required to be filed during the current year or the most recent year required to be filed.

Deductions: an expense subtracted from adjusted gross income when calculating taxable income.

Default: failure to perform a task or fulfill an obligation, especially failure to meet a financial obligation.

Delinquent return: any return required to be filed but has not been filed after the due date of the return, plus any extensions.

Dependency exemption: deduction allowed in the computation of taxable income for a person who qualifies as the taxpayer's dependent.

Dependency tests: five sets of criteria that determine whether an individual qualifies for dependent status; the five dependency tests are: (1) member of household or relationship test, (2) citizen or resident test, (3) joint return test, (4) support test, and (5) gross income test.

Dependent: a "qualifying child" or "qualifying relative," other than the taxpayer or spouse, who entitles the taxpayer to claim a dependency exemption.

Depreciation: a decrease in price or value; a noncash expense that reduces the value of an asset as a result of wear and tear, age, or obsolescence; an income tax deduction that allows a taxpayer to recover the cost of property or assets placed in service.

Discharge of federal tax lien: the removal of the United States' lien from specified property.

Dividend: a distribution of a company's earnings to a class of its shareholders.

Documentation: confirmation that some fact or statement is true through the use of documentary evidence; may also refer to the process of providing evidence.

Domicile: in law, the residence where you have your permanent home or principal establishment; your legal residence.

Dual status alien: an alien who is both a nonresident and resident alien during the same tax year; the most common dual status tax years are the years of arrival and departure.

Earned income: income derived from active participation in a trade or business, including wages, salaries, tips, commissions, bonuses, and self-employment earnings; the opposite of *unearned income*.

Earned income tax credit (EIC): a tax credit given to qualified low-income wage earners, even if no income tax was withheld from the individuals' pay.

Employee: works for an employer; employers can control when, where, and how the employee performs the work.

Enrolled agent (EA): a federally authorized tax practitioner who has technical expertise in the field of taxation and who is empowered by the U.S. Department of the Treasury to represent taxpayers before all administrative levels of the IRS for audits, collections, and appeals.

Entrepreneur: one who assumes the financial risk of the initiation, operation, and management of a given business or undertaking.

Equity: the difference between the fair market value or other value imposed and the amount owed represents the equity in a specific asset.

Estate: the net worth of a person at any point in time; the sum of a person's assets less liabilities.

Estate taxes: a tax on the estate of a person who has died; estate taxes are payable by the estate before property is transferred to heirs.

Examine (examination): the IRS term used to describe the auditing of a tax return.

Exchange: to barter, swap, part with, give, or transfer property, for other property or services.

Excludable income: income that is not included in the taxpayer's gross income and therefore exempt from federal income tax.

Executor: a legal entity, frequently an individual, known before death to a testator, who is named in the testator's will to carry out the desires of the deceased after his death as designated in the will.

Exempt (from withholding): free from withholding of federal income tax; must meet certain income, tax liability, and dependency criteria and does not exempt a person from other kinds of tax withholding.

Excise tax: a federal or state tax imposed on the manufacture and distribution of certain non-essential consumer goods, such as environmental taxes, communications taxes, and fuel taxes.

Exemptions: immunity from an obligation or duty; in regard to taxes, a deduction allowed to a taxpayer because of his or her status.

Fair market value (FMV): the price at which a willing seller will sell, and a willing buyer will buy, in an arm's length transaction when neither is under compulsion to sell or buy and both have reasonable knowledge of relevant facts.

Federal/State E-file: a program sponsored by the IRS in partnership with participating states that allows taxpayers to file federal and state income tax returns electronically at the same time.

Federal income tax: a tax levied by the federal government on the income of individuals and businesses.

Federal Insurance Contributions Act (FICA): a law requiring a deduction from paychecks and income that goes toward the Social Security program and Medicare; both employees and employers are responsible for sharing the FICA payments.

Federal Unemployment Tax Act (FUTA): provides for payments of unemployment compensation to workers who have lost their jobs; only employers pay FUTA tax.

Fiduciary: an individual or entity holding assets for another party, often with the legal authority and duty to make decisions regarding financial matters on behalf of the other party.

Filing status: determines the rate at which income is taxed (see *single, married filing jointly, married filing separate, head of household*, and *qualifying widow(er)*).

Financial records: all transaction information regarding finances; for tax purposes, spending and income records and items including paycheck stubs, statements of interest or dividends earned, records of gifts, tips, and bonuses, canceled checks, receipts, and credit card statements.

Fixed assets: those assets of a permanent nature required for the normal conduct of a business, and that will not normally be converted into cash during the ensuing fiscal period.

Fixed costs: operating expenses incurred to provide facilities and organization that are kept in readiness to do business without regard to actual volumes of production and sales.

Terms You Should Know

Forced sale value: the price at which an asset can be sold at an auction; the highest price an asset can reasonably be expected to bring if offered for sale without the consent or concurrence of the owner by virtue of judicial process under certain restrictions in terms of market or time.

Form 1040: the U.S. individual income tax return form.

Form W-2: an IRS form used to report wages earned and taxes withheld in a given year.

Form W-4: an IRS form used to collect information from employees used to calculate the correct amount of income tax to be withheld from the employees' compensation.

Garnishment: a court-ordered process that takes property from a person to pay a debt; the attachment or seizure of personal wages through a court-assisted process.

Goodwill: in business, an intangible asset valued according to the advantage or reputation a business has acquired over and above its tangible assets.

Grantor: the individual or entity that transfers property to another.

Gross income: income generated before deducting expenses, taxes, insurance, etc.

Gross profit: the difference between revenue and the cost of making a product or providing a service before deducting overhead, payroll, taxes, and interest payments.

Head of household (HOH): a U.S. income tax filing status that can be used by an unmarried person who maintains a home for a dependent during the tax year.

Includable income: income included in the taxpayer's gross income and therefore subject to federal income tax.

Income tax: taxes on income, both earned (salaries, wages, tips, commissions) and unearned (interest and dividends); income taxes can be levied both on individuals and businesses.

Independent contractor: a self-employed individual who performs services for others; the recipients of the services do not control the means or methods the contractor uses to accomplish the work.

Individual Master File (IMF): a file maintained by the IRS that contains all tax data and related information pertaining to individual personal income taxpayers intended to reflect a continuously updated and current record of each taxpayer's account.

Individual Taxpayer Identification Number (ITIN): a nine-digit number issued by the IRS to individuals who are required to have a U.S. taxpayer identification number but who do not have and are not eligible to obtain a Social Security number from the Social Security Administration.

Inflation: a general and progressive increase in prices.

Information return: a return that provides information to the tax collecting agency but does not compute the tax liability.

Innocent spouse: a spouse who unknowingly filed a joint return with their spouse who had reported an understatement of tax due to erroneous items.

Installment agreement: an agreement between the IRS and a taxpayer to allow the taxpayer to pay a tax liability over a specified period.

Integrated Data Retrieval System (IDRS): an internal IRS computer system that allows district and service center employees to have direct, online access to taxpayer accounts through computer screens.

Interest income: income received from certain financial accounts or from lending money to someone else.

Installment sale: the selling of property and receiving the sales price over a series of payments, instead of all at once at the close of the sale.

Interest income: the income a person receives from certain bank accounts or from lending money to someone else.

Interest: the charge for the use of borrowed money.

Internal Revenue Code (IRC): the body of law created by congressional action that governs the entire administrative process of the U.S. tax system.

Internal Revenue Service (IRS): the federal agency that collects income taxes in the United States.

Itemized deductions: expenses claimed on an individual's tax return that are subtracted from the adjusted gross income to determine taxable income.

Investment income: income from investments that includes taxable interest and dividends; tax-exempt interest, capital gain net income, net income from rents and royalties not derived from a trade or business, and net income from passive activities.

Joint return: a U.S. income tax filing status that can be used by a married couple.

Levy: a legal seizure of real or personal property to satisfy a tax debt; property includes real estate, vehicles, money held in bank accounts, future income, etc.

Lien: a charge or encumbrance in favor of one party or entity on the property of another party arising by reason of a debt or obligation owing from the latter to the former.

Licensed taxpayer representative (LTR): a tax professional, such as an enrolled agent, licensed to practice before the IRS.

Like kind: refers to property that is similar to another for which it has been exchanged.

Local taxes: taxes imposed by a local city or town; examples of local taxes are property taxes, sales taxes, and occasionally income taxes.

Low Income Taxpayer Clinic (LITC): an independent organization that provides low income taxpayers with representation in federal tax controversies with the IRS and assists taxpayers with limited English proficiency; services provided for free or a nominal charge.

Married filing joint status (MFJ): filing status for married couples where income and expense deductions are combined.

Married filing separate status (MFS): filing status for married couples who choose to report their respective incomes, exemptions, and deductions on separate tax returns.

Medicare: a federal program that pays for certain health care expenses for people age 65 and older.

Medicare tax: the tax paid to cover the cost of Medicare.

Minimum wage: the lowest compensation an employer is allowed to pay an employee for hourly work.

Monthly disposable income (MDI): any amount remaining after a taxpayer's necessary monthly living expenses are subtracted from monthly income.

Net income: the excess of revenues over outlays in a given period; gross profit minus operating expenses and taxes.

Net operating loss (NOL): a net loss for the year attributable to business or casualty losses; for federal income tax purposes, a net operating loss is defined as the excess of business deductions computed with certain modifications over gross income in a particular tax year.

Nonpassive income: any income that cannot be classified as passive; any type of active income such as wages, business income, or investment income.

Nonrefundable credit: a tax credit that only offsets tax liability; nonrefundable credits allow taxpayers to reduce their tax to zero but they cannot receive a refund for any excess nonrefundable credit.

Nontaxable exchange: an exchange of property in which any gain or loss realized is not recognized.

Nontaxable income: income that is not subject to tax.

Notice of Federal Tax Lien: the federal tax lien gives the IRS a legal claim to the taxpayer's property for the amount of the tax debt; filing the Notice of Federal Tax Lien establishes priority rights against certain other creditors and publicly notifies other creditors of the U.S. government's claim.

Notice of Levy: a document that apprises a debtor that a judgment creditor has applied to a court for permission to attach or levy assets or real property as a means by which to satisfy the creditor's judgment; a Notice of Levy by the IRS is notice that the IRS intends to seize property in the near future.

Offer in compromise (OIC): an agreement between the IRS and taxpayer that allows the taxpayer's delinquent tax debt to be settled for less than the amount owed.

Paid preparers: persons who are paid to prepare tax returns for others; paid preparers are legally liable under federal law for the returns they prepare, volunteers are not.

Partnership: an unincorporated business that has more than one owner.

Passive activity: one or more trade, business, or rental activity that the taxpayer does not materially participate in managing or running.

Passive income: taxable income that comes from passive activity.

Payroll taxes: taxes withheld from employee pay for federal income taxes (FIT) owed by the employee.

Payroll period: a period of service for which the employer usually pays wages.

Personal exemption: a dollar amount excluded from taxable income on one's income tax return; the personal exemption is offered to taxpayers who cannot be claimed as dependents on someone else's tax return.

Personal identification number (PIN): a secret numeric password shared between a user and a system used to authenticate the user to the system; a personal identification number established with the IRS system allows taxpayers to sign their returns electronically and ensures that electronically submitted tax returns are authentic.

Personal income tax: the tax an individual pays on their yearly total amount of taxable income.

Property taxes: taxes on property, especially real estate, but also can be on boats, automobiles, recreational vehicles, and business inventories.

Qualifying child: a category of dependent under which the dependent must meet eight tests: (1) relationship, (2) age, (3) residence, (4) support, (5) citizenship or residency, (6) joint return, (7) qualifying child of more than one person, and (8) dependent taxpayer.

Qualifying relative: a category of dependent under which the dependent must meet seven tests: (1) not a qualifying child, (2) member of household or relationship, (3) citizenship or residency, (4) gross income, (5) support, (6) joint return, and (7) dependent taxpayer.

Qualifying widow(er) filing status: a filing status that entitles the surviving spouse to use joint return tax rates and the highest standard deduction amount.

Quick sale value (QSV): price at which an individual will sell, and a willing buyer will buy, in an arm's length transaction when the seller is under compulsion or duress to sell.

Reasonable collection potential (RCP): the total realizable value of the taxpayer's assets plus any future income.

Recovery period: the period of time, normally years, over which the basis (cost) of an item of property is recovered (by depreciation).

Terms You Should Know

Refund: relative to taxes, money owed to taxpayers when their total tax payments are greater than the total tax.

Refund statute expiration date: the date by which a taxpayer may request a refund of an overpayment; the refund statute expiration date is generally within three years from the time the return was filed or within two years from the time the tax was paid, whichever is later.

Refundable credit: occurs when the amount of a credit is greater than the tax owed; taxpayers not only can have their tax reduced to zero but also receive a "refund" of excess credit.

Revenue officer (RO): an IRS employee who audits large dollar Form 1040 accounts, corporations, and other business returns; a person working for the IRS collections department.

Sales tax: a tax on retail products based on a set percentage of retail cost.

Schedule C–Profit and Loss from Business: form used when a taxpayer has an unincorporated business and is a sole proprietor business owner; allows taxpayers to deduct the expenses incurred during the tax year they conducted business from the gross income received.

Schedule K-1–Partner's Share of Income, Credit, and Deductions: form used by each partner in the partnership to report his or her share of the partnership incomes, credits, deductions, etc.

Self-employment income: earned income from a trade, business, farming, or profession not paid by an employer.

Self-employment tax: the Social Security and Medicare tax paid by people who work for themselves.

Self-releasing lien: a lien that releases automatically after a period of time; in the case of federal tax liens, the Notice of Federal Tax Lien clearly states the self-releasing conditions.

Single filing status: filing status for unmarried individuals, or those who are legally separated from their spouse.

Social Security tax: a tax that provides benefits for retired workers and their dependents, as well as for the disabled and their dependents.

Sole proprietorship: a form of business organization with specific, distinguishing characteristics such as only one owner for the business and the business is unincorporated.

Standard deduction: amount the IRS will allow to be subtracted from the adjusted gross income to determine taxable income, based on filing status.

Standard mileage method: one of two methods (the other is *actual expense method*) of calculating business automobile expenses; the taxpayer multiplies the business miles driven by the mileage rate for that tax year.

Status 53: when a taxpayer is unable to pay his or her tax liability and collection activity would create an economic hardship, the IRS will consider classifying the taxpayer's account as Status 53 or currently not collectible.

Subordination of federal tax lien: legal process whereby the IRS will subordinate its federal tax lien to a third party by temporarily setting aside the lien to enable a refinance or sale of a piece of property.

Substitute for return (SFR): a tax return filed by the IRS when a taxpayer has not filed.

Tax avoidance: the use of legal methods to modify an individual's financial situation to lower the amount of income tax owed.

Tax Code: the official body of tax laws and regulations.

Tax credit: a dollar-for-dollar reduction in tax liability.

Tax cut: a reduction in taxes.

Tax deductions: an amount that reduces income subject to tax.

Terms You Should Know

Tax evasion: a failure to pay or a deliberate underpayment of taxes; tax evasion is illegal.

Tax exempt: not subject to tax.

Tax gap: the difference between the amount of tax that taxpayers should pay and the amount paid voluntarily and on time; the tax gap can also be thought of as the sum of non-compliance with the tax law.

Tax liability: the amount of tax owed; taxpayers meet or pay their federal income tax liability through withholding, estimated tax payments, and payments made with the tax forms they file with the government.

Tax return: reports filed with the IRS or state or local tax collection agencies containing information used to calculate income tax and other taxes.

Tax shift: the process that occurs when a tax levied on one person or group is in fact paid by others.

Taxes: required payments of money to governments used to provide public goods and services for the benefit of the community as a whole.

Taxpayer delinquency investigation (TDI): delinquent unfiled return investigation.

Taxpayer delinquent account (TDA): a balance due module for a specific taxpayer.

TIN: Taxpayer identification number.

Trustee: in bankruptcy cases, the individual appointed by the court to assume control of the bankrupt's assets for orderly liquidation (see also *fiduciary*).

Underground economy: money-making activities not reported to the government and therefore not taxed, including illegal and legal activities.

Unearned income: income other than pay for work performed; interest and dividends from savings or investments are common types of unearned income.

Unemployment Insurance or Compensation (UIC or UEC): a state program that requires employers to pay a percentage of gross wages to fund the payment of unemployment compensation for individuals who have become unemployed.

Value: the amount of money or goods or services considered to be a fair equivalent for something else.

Voluntary compliance: a system of compliance that relies on individual citizens to report their income freely and voluntarily, calculate their tax liability correctly, and file a tax return on time.

Volunteer Income Tax Assistance (VITA): an IRS program that provides free income tax return preparation for certain taxpayers.

Wages: compensation received by employees for services performed.

Withholding: money that employers withhold from employees' paychecks and deposit for the federal government to be credited against the employees' tax liability when they file their returns.

Withholding allowance: claimed by an employee on Form W-4; an employer uses the number of allowances claimed, together with income earned and marital status, to determine how much income tax to withhold from wages.

Acronyms and Abbreviations

Listen to one or more tax professionals talk, and you'll rapidly conclude that their vocabulary bears more resemblance to alphabet soup than English. These are some of the acronyms and abbreviations you are likely to hear as you work through your tax issues.

ACS: Automated collection system

AGI: Adjusted gross income

CAF: Centralized authorization file

CDP: Collection due process

CIS: Collection Information Statement

CID: Criminal Investigation Division

COGS: Cost of goods sold

EIC: Earned income credit

EITC: Earned Income Tax Credit

EA: Enrolled agent

FMV: Fair market value

FICA: Federal Insurance Contributions Act

FUTA: Federal Unemployment Tax Act

HOH: Head of household

IA: Installment agreement

IMF: Individual Master File

ITIN: Individual Taxpayer Identification Number

IDRS: Integrated Data Retrieval System

IRC: Internal Revenue Code

IRS: Internal Revenue Service

LITC: Low Income Taxpayer Clinic

LTR: Licensed taxpayer representative

MFJ: Married filing jointly

MFS: Married filing separately

MDI: Monthly disposable income

NOL: Net operating loss

OIC: Offer in compromise

PIN: Personal identification number

QSV: Quick Sale Value

RCP: Reasonable collection potential

RO: Revenue officer

SOC: Stay of collections

SFR: Substitute for return

TCO: Tax compliance officer

TDA: Taxpayer delinquent account

TDI: Taxpayer delinquency investigation

TIN: Taxpayer Identification Number

TFRP: Trust Fund Recovery Penalty

UIC/UEC: Unemployment Insurance or Compensation

VITA: Volunteer Income Tax Assistance

State Departments of Revenue Contact Information

Alabama

Alabama Department of Revenue
www.ador.state.al.us
Physical address:
50 N. Ripley
Montgomery, AL 36132
Collections address:
Collection Services Division
P.O. Box 327820
Montgomery, AL 36132-7820

Address for payments:
Alabama Department of Revenue
P.O. Box 2401
Montgomery, AL 36140-0001
Address for mailing return:
Alabama Department of Revenue
P.O. Box 154
Montgomery, AL 36135-0001
General information: (334) 242-1170
Collection services: (334) 242-1220

Collections fax: (334) 242-8342
Tax fraud hotline: (800) 535-9410
Income tax refund: (800) 558-3912
TTY number: (334) 242-3061
Use contact form online to contact via e-mail.

Taxpayer Service Centers

Auburn-Opelika Taxpayer Service Center
Physical address:
3300 Skyway Dr.
Auburn, AL 36830
Mailing address:
P.O. Box 2929
Auburn, AL 36831-2929
Phone: (334) 887-9549
Fax: (334) 887-9885

Jefferson/Shelby Taxpayer Service Center
Physical address:
2020 Valleydale Rd., Suite 208
Hoover, AL 35244
Mailing address:
P.O. Box 1927
Pelham, AL 35124
Phone: (205) 733-2740
Fax: (205) 733-2989

Dothan Taxpayer Service Center
Physical address:
344 North Oates St.
Dothan, AL 36303
Mailing address:
P.O. Box 5739
Dothan, AL 36302-5739
Phone: (334) 793-5803
Fax: (334) 793-1488

Gadsden Taxpayer Service Center
Physical address:
235 College St.

Gadsden, AL 35901
Mailing address:
P.O. Drawer 1190
Gadsden, AL 35902-1190
Phone: (256) 547-0554
Fax: (256) 547-6922

Huntsville Taxpayer Service Center
Physical address:
4920 Corporate Dr., Suite H
Huntsville, AL 35805-6204
Mailing address:
P.O. Box 11487
Huntsville, AL 35814
Phone: (256) 837-2319
Fax: (256) 837-7322

Mobile Taxpayer Service Center
Physical address:
955 Downtowner Blvd.
Mobile, AL 36609
Mailing address:
P.O. Drawer 160406
Mobile, AL 36616-1406
Phone: (251) 344-4737
Fax: (251) 342-2054

Montgomery Taxpayer Service Center
Physical address:
1021 Madison Ave.
Montgomery, AL 36104
Mailing address:
P.O. Box 327490
Montgomery, AL 36132-7490
Phone: (334) 242-2677
Fax: (334) 265-9887

Muscle Shoals Office
Physical address:
874 Reservation Rd.

Muscle Shoals, AL 35662
Mailing address:
P.O. Box 3148
Muscle Shoals, AL 35662
Phone: (256) 383-4631
Fax: (256) 381-7200

Tuscaloosa Taxpayer Service Center
Physical address:
518 19th Ave.
Tuscaloosa, AL 35401
Mailing address:
P.O. Box 2467
Tuscaloosa, AL 35403-2467
Phone: (205) 759-2571
Fax: (205) 349-3780

Alaska

Alaska Department of Revenue
www.revenue.state.ak.us
Juneau Commissioner's Office
P.O. Box 110400
333 W. Willoughby, 11th Floor SOB
Juneau, AK 99811-0400
Anchorage Commissioner's Office
550 W. 7th Ave., Suite 1820
Anchorage, AK 99501
General information: (907) 465-2300

Arizona

Arizona Department of Revenue
www.azdor.gov
Physical address:
State of Arizona Department of Revenue
1600 W. Monroe
Phoenix, AZ 85007-2650

Mailing addresses:

Individual Income Tax Returns (Refund/No Payment)
P.O. Box 52138
Phoenix, AZ 85072-2138
Barcode Returns:
P.O. Box 29205
Phoenix, AZ 85038-9205

Individual Income Tax Returns (with Payment)
P.O. Box 52016
Phoenix, AZ 85072-2016
Barcode Returns:
P.O. Box 29204
Phoenix, AZ 85038-9204
Collections Section:
P.O. Box 29070
Phoenix, AZ 85038-9070

Tax Assistance
Individual/Corporate Income Taxes: (602) 255-3381
Toll Free from 520 or 928 area code: (800) 352-4090
TTY/TDD: (602) 542-4021
Collections: (602) 542-5551
East Valley: (480) 545-3500
Tucson: (520) 628-6442
Field Collections Fax: (602) 716-7971
East Phoenix Metro Area Office:
275 E. Germann Rd., Bldg. 2, Suite 180
Gilbert, AZ 85297-2917
Tucson Office:
400 W. Congress
Tucson, AZ 85701

Arkansas

Arkansas Department of Finance and Administration
www.state.ar.us/dfa/dfa_taxes.html

Individual Income Tax
Ledbetter Building
1816 W. 7th St., Room 2300
Little Rock, AR 72201
Mailing address:
P.O. Box 3628
Little Rock, AR 72203

Field Audit Administration
Phone: (501) 682-4616
Fax: (501) 683-2082
General: (501) 682-1100
Fax: (501) 682-7692
Income Tax Administration:
Phone: (501) 682-1130
Fax: (501) 682-1691

California

Franchise Tax Board
www.ftb.ca.gov
Refund, Zero Balance, or Balance Due without Payment:
Returns: 540, 540A, 540 2EZ, 540NR, 540X
Franchise Tax Board
P.O. Box 942840
Sacramento, CA 94240-0002

Payment with Return
Returns: 540, 540A, 540 2EZ, 540NR, 540X
Franchise Tax Board
P.O. Box 942867
Sacramento, CA 94267-0001
Refund, Zero Balance, or Balance Due without Payment:
Returns: Scannable Returns 540
Franchise Tax Board
P.O. Box 942840
Sacramento, CA 94240-0009

Payment with Return
Returns: Scannable Returns 540

State Departments of Revenue Contact Information

Franchise Tax Board
P.O. Box 942867
Sacramento, CA 94267-0009
General information: (800) 852-5711
Automated service: (800) 338-0505
TTY/TDD: (800) 822-6268
Private Collection Agency: (916) 845-5992
Notice RE Referral to Private Collection Agency: (916) 845-5085
Collection Contact Center: (800) 689-4776 or (916) 845-4470

California Employment Development Department
www.edd.ca.gov

General questions or comments
Employment Development Department
P.O. Box 826880, MIC 83
Sacramento, CA 94280-0001
Disability Insurance: (800) 480-3287
Paid Family Leave: (877) 238-4373
Unemployment Services: (866) 333-4606
CSR (Unemployment): (800) 300-5616
Payroll Tax Assistance: (888) 745-3886
Disability Insurance (TTY): (800) 563-2441
Employment Tax (TTY): (800) 547-9565
Unemployment Insurance (TTY): (800) 815-9387

California Board of Equalization
www.boe.ca.gov
Mailing address:
State Board of Equalization
P.O. Box 942879
Sacramento, CA 94279
21 District Offices Available (all listed on the website)
General Tax Questions: (800) 400-7115
Tax Practitioner Hotline: (800) 401-3661
Taxpayers' Rights Advocate: (888) 324-2798

Colorado

Colorado Department of Revenue
www.colorado.gov/revenue
Primary Taxation Mailing Address:
Colorado Department of Revenue
1375 Sherman St.
Denver, CO 80261

Colorado Springs Regional Service Center
2447 N. Union Blvd.
Colorado Springs, CO 80909

Fort Collins Service Center
1121 W. Prospect Rd., Bldg. D
Fort Collins, CO 80526

Grand Junction Service Center
222 S. 6th St., Room 208
Grand Junction, CO 81501

Pueblo Service Center
827 W. 4th St., Suite A
Pueblo, CO 81003

Customer Service: (303) 238-7378
Income Tax Account and Refund Info: (303) 238-3278
TTY Telephone Users: (800) 659-2656
Voice Telephone Users: (800) 659-3656
EFT/Electronic Payment Help: (303) 205-8333
Office Collections: (303) 205-8291

Connecticut

Connecticut Department of Revenue Services
www.ct.gov/drs/site/default.asp
Main Office:
Department of Revenue Services
Taxpayer Services Division
25 Sigourney St., Suite 2
Hartford, CT 06106

State Departments of Revenue Contact Information 161

Telephone Assistance: (860) 297-5962 (from anywhere) or (800) 382-9463 (within CT, outside Greater Hartford area only)
TDD/TTY: (860) 297-4911

Delaware

State of Delaware Division of Revenue
http://revenue.delaware.gov

New Castle County
Carvel State Office Building
820 North French St.
Wilmington, DE 19801
Phone: (302) 577-8200
Fax: (302) 577-8202

Kent County
Thomas Collins Building
540 S. Dupont Hwy.
Dover, DE 19901
Phone: (302) 744-1085
Fax: (302) 744-1095

Sussex County
20653 Dupont Blvd., Suite 2
Georgetown, DE 19947
Phone: (302) 856-5358
Fax: (302) 856-5697

Personal Income Tax Assistance: (302) 577-8200
E-mail: personaltax@state.de.us
Business Tax Assistance: (302) 577-8205
E-mail: Bus Tax Information: michael.x.smith@state.de.us
Collections/Account Management: (302) 577-8785
Note: Contact information for individuals within the departments (phone and e-mail) can be found on the website

District of Columbia

Office of Tax and Revenue

otr.cfo.dc.gov/otr/site/default.asp
Office of Tax and Revenue
Customer Service Center
1101 4th St., SW, Suite W270
Washington, DC 20024
Phone: (202) 727-4TAX
Fax: (202) 442-6304

Collection Division Contact Information
Office of Tax and Revenue
Compliance Administration
Collection Division
1101 4th St., SW
Washington, DC 20024
Phone: (202) 724-5045 or (202) 727-4829
Fax: (202) 442-6885
Mailing address:
Office of Tax and Revenue
Compliance Administration
Collection Division
P.O. Box 37559
Washington, DC 20013
Note: List of contacts, phone numbers, and e-mails can be found on the website

Florida

www.myflorida.com/dor
Florida Department of Revenue
5050 West Tennessee St.
Tallahassee, FL 32399-0100
E-mail: EMailDOR@dor.state.fl.us
Phone: (800) 352-3671
Taxpayer Rights Office
P.O. Box 5906
Tallahassee, FL 32314-5906
Phone: (850) 617-8168

Technical Assistance and Dispute Resolution
P.O. Box 7443
Tallahassee, FL 32314-7443
Phone: (850) 617-8346

General Tax Administration
5050 W. Tennessee St., D-1
Tallahassee, FL 32399-0100
Phone: (800) 352-3671

Property Tax Oversight
Florida Department of Revenue
P.O. Box 3000
Tallahassee, FL 32315-3000
Phone: (850) 717-6570

Georgia

Georgia Department of Revenue
www.etax.dor.ga.gov
Address:
1800 Century Blvd., NE
Atlanta GA 30345-3205
Phone: (877) 423-6711

Compliance for Individuals
1800 Century Blvd., NE
Atlanta, GA 30345
Phone: (404) 417-6400
Fax: (404) 417-6551
Collections: (404) 417-6340

Individual Taxes
1800 Century Blvd., Room 8300
Atlanta, GA 30345
Phone: (404) 417-2400
Fax: (404) 417-2439
E-mail: taxpayer.services@dor.ga.gov

Hawaii

State of Hawaii Department of Taxation
www.state.hi.us/tax
Mailing address:
State of Hawaii Department of Taxation
P.O. Box 259
Honolulu, HI 96809-0259

Oahu District Office
Princess Ruth Keelikolani Building
830 Punchbowl St.
Honolulu, HI 96813-5094
Phone: (808) 587-4242 or (800) 222-3229
Hearing-impaired: (808) 587-1418 or (900) 887-8974
Fax: (808) 587-1488

Maui District Office
State Office Building
54 S. High St., #208
Wailuku, HI 96793-2198

Hawaii District Office
State Office Building
75 Aupuni St., #101
Hilo, HI 96720-4245

Kauai District Office
State Office Building
3060 Eiwa St., #105
Lihue, HI 96766-1889

Idaho

Idaho State Tax Commission
http://tax.idaho.gov/index.html
Mailing address:
Idaho State Tax Commission
P.O. Box 36
Boise ID 83722-0410

State Departments of Revenue Contact Information

Office Locations

Boise
800 Park Blvd.
Plaza IV
Boise, ID 83712-7742

Coeur d'Alene
1910 Northwest Blvd., Suite 100
Coeur d'Alene, ID 83814-2371

Idaho Falls
150 Shoup Ave., Suite 16
Idaho Falls, ID 83402-3657

Lewiston
1118 F St.
Lewiston, ID 83501-1014

Pocatello
611 Wilson Ave., Suite 5
Pocatello, ID 83201-5046

Twin Falls
440 Falls Ave.
Twin Falls, ID 83301-3320
Phone: (208) 334-7660 or (800) 972-7660
Hearing-impaired: (800) 377-3529

Illinois

Illinois Revenue
http://tax.illinois.gov/index.htm

Chicago
James R. Thompson Center – Concourse Level
100 W. Randolph St.
Chicago, IL 60601-3274
Phone: (800) 732-8866

Des Plaines
Maine North Regional Building
9511 Harrison Ave.

Des Plaines, IL 60016-1563
Phone: (847) 294-4200

Fairview Heights
15 Executive Dr., Suite 2
Fairview Heights, IL 62208-1331
Phone: (618) 624-6773

Marion
2309 W. Main St., Suite 114
Marion, IL 62959-1196
Phone: (618) 993-7650

Rockford
200 S. Wyman St.
Rockford, IL 61101
Phone: (815) 987-5210

Springfield
Willard Ice Building
101 W. Jefferson St.
Springfield, IL 62702
Phone: (800) 732-8866 or (217) 782-3336
Telephone Assistance: (800) 732-8866 or (217) 782-3336
TDD: (800) 544-5304
Problems Resolution Division: (217) 785-7313

Indiana

Indiana Department of Revenue
www.in.gov/core/taxes.html
General Inquiries:
Indiana Department of Revenue
100 N. Senate Ave.
Indianapolis, IN 46204
Individual Income Tax: (317) 232-2240
Collections: (317) 232-2165
Refund or Collection/Liability Status (Automated): (317) 233-4018

State Departments of Revenue Contact Information

Iowa

Iowa Department of Revenue
www.iowa.gov/tax
Mailing addresses:
Iowa Department of Revenue
Hoover State Office Building
1305 E. Walnut
Des Moines, IA 50319

Receiving Refund/No Tax Due
Iowa Income Tax Refund Processing
Hoover State Office Bldg.
Des Moines, IA 50319-0120

Paying Additional Tax
Iowa Income Tax
Document Processing
P.O. Box 9187
Des Moines, IA 50306-9187

About Iowa Tax Law: (515) 281-3114 or (800) 367-3388 (Iowa Only)
About eFile and Pay: (515) 281-8453 or (866) 503-3453 (Iowa Only)
Check on Your Refund: (515) 281-4966 or (800) 572-3944 (Iowa Only)
Billing and Collections: (515) 281-6944 or (866) 339-7912

Kansas

Kansas Department of Revenue
www.ksrevenue.org/index.htm
Customer Relations Contact:
Office location:
Docking State Office Building, Room 150
915 SW Harrison St.
Topeka, KS 66612

Compliance Enforcement – Collections
Docking State Office Building, Room 300
915 SW Harrison St.
Topeka, KS 66612

Kansas Tax Assistance: (785) 368-8222
Kansas Tax Form Requests (voicemail): (785) 296-4937
Collections: (785) 296-6121
Fax: (785) 291-3616
Tax Appeals: (785) 296-8460
Fax: (785) 291-3614
Hearing Impaired TTY: (785) 296-6461
E-mail: tac@kdor.state.ks.us

Kentucky

Kentucky Department of Revenue
http://revenue.ky.gov
Mailing address:
Kentucky Department of Revenue
501 High St.
Frankfort, KY 40601-2103

Taxpayer Service Centers

Ashland
134 16th St.
Ashland, KY 41101-7670
Phone: (606) 920-2037
Fax: (606) 920-2039

Bowling Green
201 W, Professional Park Ct.
Bowling Green, KY 42104-3278
Phone: (270) 746-7470
Fax: (270) 746-7847

Central Kentucky
501 High St., Station 38
Frankfort, KY 40601
Phone: (502) 564-5930
Fax: (502) 564-8946

Corbin
15100 N. US 25 E, Suite 2
Corbin, KY 40701-6188
Phone: (606) 528-3322

Fax: (606) 523-1972

Hopkinsville
181 Hammond Dr.
Hopkinsville, KY 42240-7926
Phone: (270) 889-6521
Fax: (270) 889-6563

Louisville
600 West Cedar St., 2nd Floor West
Louisville, KY 40202-2310
Phone: (502) 595-4512
Fax: (502) 595-4205

Northern Kentucky
Turfway Ridge Office Park
7310 Turfway Rd., Suite 190
Florence, KY 41042-4871
Phone: (859) 371-9049
Fax: (859) 371-9154

Owensboro
311 West 2nd St.
Owensboro, KY 42301-0734
Phone: (270) 687-7301
Fax: (270) 687-7244

Paducah
Clark Business Complex, Suite G
2928 Park Ave.
Paducah, KY 42001-4024
Phone: (270) 575-7148
Fax: (270) 575-7027

Pikeville
Uniplex Center, Suite 203
126 Trivette Dr.
Pikeville, KY 41501-1275
Phone: (606) 433-7675
Fax: (606) 433-7679

Individual Income Tax: (502) 564-4581
Collections: (502) 564-4921

Louisiana

Louisiana Department of Revenue
www.rev.state.la.us
Physical address:
Headquarters
617 N Third St.
Baton Rouge, LA 70802
Mailing address:
P.O. Box 201
Baton Rouge, LA 70821

Revenue Offices:

Alexandria
900 Murray St., Room B 100
Alexandria, LA 71309-7661

Dallas
4100 Spring Valley Rd., Suite 315
Dallas, TX 75244-3800

Houston
5177 Richmond Ave., Suite 325
Houston, TX 77056-6704

Lafayette
825 Kaliste Saloom Rd.
Brandywine III, Suite 150
Lafayette, LA 70508-4237

Lake Charles
1 Lake Shore Dr., Suite 1550
Lake Charles, LA 70629-0001

Monroe
122 St. John St., Room 105
Monroe, LA 71201-7338

New Orleans
1555 Poydras St., Suite 2100
New Orleans, LA 70112-3707

State Departments of Revenue Contact Information

Shreveport
1525 Fairfield Ave., Room 630
Shreveport, LA 71101-4371

Call Center:
Individual Taxes: (225) 219-0102
Business Taxes: (225) 219-7462
TDD: (225) 219-2114
Collection Division: (225) 219-2244

Maine

Maine Revenue Services
www.maine.gov/revenue
Mailing address:
Compliance Division/Income Division
24 State House Station
Augusta, ME 04333-0024
General information: (207) 287-2076

Collections, Payment Arrangements
Income Tax: (800) 987-7735 or (207) 621-4300
Compliance Division: (207) 624-9595
E-mail: compliance.tax@maine.gov
Income Division: (207) 626-8475
E-mail: income.tax@maine.gov

Maryland

Comptroller of Maryland
www.marylandtaxes.com

Locations

Annapolis
Revenue Administration Center
80 Calvert St.
Annapolis, MD 21404
Phone: (410) 260-7980
Phone: (800) MD-TAXES

Baltimore
State Office Bldg.
301 W. Preston St., Room 206
Baltimore, MD 21201-2384
Phone: (410) 767-1995

Cumberland
112 Baltimore St., 2nd Floor
Cumberland, MD 21502-2302
Phone: (301) 777-2165 or (301) 334-8880

Elkton
Upper Chesapeake Corporate Center
103 Chesapeake Blvd., Suite D
Elkton, MD 21921-6313
Phone: (410) 996-0580

Frederick
Courthouse/Multiservice Center
100 W. Patrick St., Room 2110
Frederick, MD 21701-5646
Phone: (301) 600-1982

Hagerstown
Professional Arts Bldg.
One S. Potomac St.
Hagerstown, MD 21740-5512
Phone: (301) 791-4776

Landover
Treetops Bldg.
8181 Professional Pl., Suite 101
Landover, MD 20785-2226
Phone: (410) 321-2306

Salisbury
State Multiservice Center
201 Baptist St., Room 2248
Salisbury, MD 21801-4961
Phone: (410) 713-3660

Towson
Hampton Plaza
300 E. Joppa Rd., Plaza Level 1A
Towson, MD 21286
Phone: (410) 321-2306

Upper Marlboro
Prince George's County Courthouse
14735 Main St., Room 083B
Upper Marlboro, MD 20772-9978
Phone: (301) 952-2810
Charles Co. residents: (301) 645-2226
D.C. Metro area: (301) 843-0977

Waldorf
1036 Saint Nicholas Dr., Suite 202
Waldorf, MD 20603
Phone: (301) 645-2226
D.C. metro area residents: (301) 843-0977

Wheaton
Wheaton Park Office Complex
11510 Georgia Ave., Suite 190
Wheaton, MD 20902-1958
Phone: (301) 949-6030

Massachusetts

Massachusetts Department of Revenue
www.mass.gov/dor

District Office Counter Locations
19 Staniford St.
Boston, MA 02114
218 S. Main St.
Fall River, MA 02721
60 Perseverance Way
Hyannis, MA 02601
333 East St.
Pittsfield, MA 01201

436 Dwight St.
Springfield, MA 01103
67 Millbrook St.
Worcester, MA 01606

Main information lines: (617) 887-MDOR or (800) 392-6089
Taxpayer Advocate: (617) 626-2201
Problem Resolution Office: (617) 626-3833
Collections Bureau: (617) 887-6400
Customer Service Bureau: (617) 887-MDOR (6367)
Toll-free in Massachusetts: (800) 392-6089

Michigan

State of Michigan Department of Treasury
www.michigan.gov/treasury
Mailing address:
Michigan Department of Treasury
Lansing, MI 48922

Collections
Michigan Department of Treasury
Collection Division
P.O. Box 30199
Lansing, MI 48909

Garnishments
Serve Garnishments by mailing to:
Michigan Department of Treasury
Third Party Withholding Unit
P.O. Box 30785
Lansing, MI 48909

General Info: (517) 373-3200
TTY: (800) 649-3777
Collections: (517) 636-5265
Fax: (517) 636-5245
Garnishments: (517) 636-5333

Garnishments/Levies – Tax Refunds and Magnetic Media
Phone: (517) 636-5333

Fax: (517) 636-5349

Garnishments/Levies – Payroll and Vendor
Phone: (517) 636-5333
Fax: (517) 636-5349

Minnesota

Minnesota Revenue
www.taxes.state.mn.us
Physical address:
Minnesota Department of Revenue
600 N. Robert St.
St. Paul, MN 55101
Individual Income Tax: (651) 296-3781 or (800) 652-9094
E-mail: indinctax@state.mn.us
Balance Due: (651) 556-3003 or (800) 657-3909
Collection Division: (651) 556-3003 or (800) 657-3909
E-mail: mdor.collection@state.mn.us

Mississippi

State of Mississippi Department of Revenue
www.dor.ms.gov
Physical address:
1577 Springridge Rd.
Raymond, MS 39154-9602
Mailing address:
P.O. Box 1033
Jackson, MS 39215-1033

District Offices

Brookhaven District
1385 Johnny Johnson Dr.
P.O. Box 3999
Brookhaven, MS 39603-7999
Phone: (601) 833-4761
Fax: (601) 833-3096

Greenwood District
117 B Grand Blvd.
P.O. Drawer D
Greenwood, MS 38935-0420
Phone: (662) 453-1742
Fax: (662) 453-7981

Gulf Coast District
1141 Bayview Ave.
Biloxi, MS 39530-1601
Phone: (228) 436-0554

Hattiesburg District
17 JM Taturn Industrial Dr.
P.O. Box 1709
Hattiesburg, MS 39403-1709
Phone: (601) 545-1261
Fax: (601) 584-4051

Jackson District
1577 Springridge Rd.
P.O. Box 1033
Jackson, MS 39215-1033
Phone: (601) 923-7300
Fax: (601) 923-7318

Meridian District
1577 Springridge Rd.
P.O. Box 1033
Jackson, MS 39215-1033
Phone: (601) 483-2273
Fax: (601) 693-2473

Senatobia District
2778 Hwy. 51 South
P.O. Box 127
Senatobia, MS 38668
Phone: (662) 562-4489
Fax: (662) 562-7392

Tupelo District
2610 Traceland Dr.

State Departments of Revenue Contact Information

P.O. Box 3000
Tupelo, MS 38803
Phone: (662) 842-4316
Fax: (662) 842-5041

Tax Liens, Levies, Attachments, or Garnishments
Mississippi Department of Revenue–Collection Division
Mailing address:
P.O. Box 23338
Jackson, MS 39225-3338
Phone: (601) 923-7000

Tax Liens, Levies, Attachments, or Garnishments
Mississippi Department of Revenue–Collection Division
Phone: (601) 923-7390
Income Tax Liens: (601) 923-7391
Fax: (601) 923-7334

Missouri
Missouri Department of Revenue
http://dor.mo.gov
Central Office:
Harry S Truman State Office Building
301 W. High St.
Jefferson City, MO 65101

Individual Income Tax
Refund or No Balance Due:
Individual Income Tax
P.O. Box 500
Jefferson City, MO 65106-0500

Owe Balance Due:
Individual Income Tax
P.O. Box 329
Jefferson City, MO 65107-0329

2D Barcode Returns
Refund or No Balance Due:
Individual Income Tax
P.O. Box 3222

Jefferson City, MO 65105-3222

Owe Balance Due:
Individual Income Tax
P.O. Box 3370
Jefferson City, MO 65105-3370
Phone: (573) 751-3505

Automated Inquiry: (573) 526-8299
Billings: (573) 751-7200
Fax: (573) 751-2195
Speech/Hearing Impairment: (800) 735-2966
Individual Income Tax: income@dor.mo.gov

Montana

Montana Department of Revenue
http://revenue.mt.gov/default.mcpx
Physical address:
Sam W. Mitchell Bldg.
125 N. Roberts, 3rd Floor
Helena, MT
Mailing address:
Individual Income Tax Returns with Payments
P.O. Box 6308
Helena, MT 59604

With Refund Request or Zero Balance
P.O. Box 6577
Helena, MT 59604

Garnishments and Wage Levies
P.O. Box 6308
Helena, MT 59604

Toll-free: (866) 859-2254
In Helena: (406) 444-6900
TDD: (406) 444-2830

Nebraska

Nebraska Department of Revenue
www.revenue.ne.gov

Omaha
Nebraska State Office Bldg.
1313 Farnam St.
Omaha, NE 68102-1871
Phone: (402) 595-2065

Lincoln
Nebraska State Office Building
301 Centennial Mall South
P.O. Box 94818
Lincoln, NE 68509-4818
Phone: (402) 471-5729

Toll Free (NE and IA): (800) 742-7474
TDD: (800) 382-9309

Nevada

Nevada Department of Taxation
http://tax.state.nv.us
1550 College Parkway
Carson City, NV 89706

Carson City
Phone: (775) 684-2000
Fax: (775) 684-2020

Las Vegas
Phone: (702) 486-2300
Fax: (702) 486-2373

Henderson
Phone: (702) 486-2300
Fax: (702) 486-3377

Reno
Phone: (775) 687-9999
Fax: (775) 688-1303

New Hampshire

New Hampshire Department of Revenue Administration
www.nh.gov/revenue
Administration Unit
109 Pleasant St.
P.O. Box 457
Concord, NH 03302-0457
Phone: (603) 271-2318

Discovery Bureau
P.O. Box 488
Concord, NH 03302-0488
Phone: (603) 271-8454

Hearings Bureau
P.O. Box 1467
Concord, NH 03302-1467
Phone: (603) 271-1304

Central Taxpayer Services
109 Pleasant St.
Concord, NH 0330
Phone: (603) 271-2191

Audit Division
P.O. Box 457
Concord, NH 03302-0457
Phone: (603) 271-3400
Fax: (603) 271-6146

Collection Division
P.O. Box 454
Concord, NH 03302-0454
Phone: (603) 271-3701
Fax: (603) 271-1756

Document Processing Division
P.O. Box 637
Concord, NH 03302-0637
Phone: (603) 271-2191

New Jersey

State of New Jersey Department of the Treasury – Division of Taxation
www.state.nj.us/treasury/taxation
Mailing address:
State of New Jersey
NJ Division of Taxation
Information and Publications Branch
P.O. Box 281
Trenton, NJ 08695-0281

Regional Offices

Camden
2 Riverside Dr., Suite 20
Camden, NJ 08103

Fair Lawn
22-08 Route 208 South
Fair Lawn, NJ 07410

Neptune Regional Office
1828 W. Lake Ave., 3rd Floor
Neptune, NJ 07753

Newark
124 Halsey St., 2nd Floor
Newark, NJ 07102

Northfield
1915-A New Rd., Route 9
Northfield, NJ 08225

Somerville
75 Veterans Memorial Dr. East, Suite 103
Somerville, NJ 08876

Trenton
Taxation Bldg.
50 Barrack St., 1st Floor Lobby
Trenton, NJ 08695

Quakerbridge
Quakerbridge Plaza Office Complex
Quakerbridge Rd., Bldg. 5, 3rd Floor
Mercerville, NJ 08619

General Tax Information: (609) 826-4400 or (800) 323-4400 (within NJ, NY, PA, DE, MD)
Main Customer Service Center: (609) 292-6400
TTY/TDD: (609) 984-7300 or (800) 286-6613 (within NJ, NY, PA, DE, MD)

New Mexico

New Mexico Taxation and Revenue Department
www.tax.state.nm.us
Mailing address:
Personal Income Tax (PIT) Correspondence
P.O. Box 2788
Santa Fe, NM 87504-2788

Tax Compliance Bureau
P.O. Box 8575
Albuquerque, NM 87198-8575
General address:
1100 S. St. Francis Dr.
Santa Fe, NM 87504-0630
Phone: (505) 827-0700

District Field Offices

Albuquerque District Office
5301 Central Ave. NE
Albuquerque, NM 87198-8485
Phone: (505) 841-6200

Roswell District Office
400 Pennsylvania Ave., Suite 200
Roswell, NM 88202-1557
Phone: (575) 624-6065

Santa Fe District Office
1200 S. St. Francis Dr.
Santa Fe, NM 87502-5374
Phone: (505) 827-0951

Farmington District Office
3501 E. Main St., Suite N
Farmington, NM 87499-0479
Phone: (505) 325-5049

Las Cruces District Office
2540 S. El Paseo, Bldg. #2
Las Cruces, NM 88004-0607
Phone: (575) 524-6225

New York

New York State Department of Taxation and Finance
www.tax.state.ny.us
Mailing address:

Bills
NYS Assessment Receivables
P.O. Box 4127
Binghamton, NY 13902-4127
Personal Income Tax Return

No Payment
State Processing Center
P.O. Box 61000
Albany, NY 12261-0001

With Payment
State Processing Center
P.O. Box 15555
Albany, NY 12212-5555

District Office Locations

Binghamton District Office
44 Hawley St., 8th Floor
Binghamton, NY 13901-4480

Buffalo District Office
77 Broadway
Buffalo, NY 14203

Capital Region District Office
One Broadway Center, 9th Floor
Schenectady, NY 12305

Metropolitan District Office
55 Hanson Place
Brooklyn, NY 11217

Nassau District Office
400 Oak St.
Garden City, NY 11530

Queens District Office
80-02 Kew Gardens Rd., 5th Floor
Kew Gardens, NY 11415

Rochester District Office
340 East Main St.
Rochester, NY 14604

Suffolk District Office
State Office Bldg., Room 1B3
Veterans Memorial Hwy.
Hauppauge, NY 11788

Syracuse District Office
333 E. Washington St.
Syracuse, NY 13202

Utica District Office
207 Genesee St.
Utica, NY 13501

Westchester District Office
90 S. Ridge St.
Rye Brook, NY 10573

Midwestern Regional Office
1011 E. Touhy Ave., Suite 475
Des Plaines, IL 60018

State Departments of Revenue Contact Information

Manhattan District Office
1740 Broadway
New York, NY 10019-4357

Tax Refund Info: (518) 457-5149
Disagree with Personal Income Tax Bill: (518) 485-9791
Disagree with Personal Income Tax Adjusted Refund: (518) 485-6549
Personal Income Tax Information Center: (518) 457-5181
Collections and Civil Enforcement Division: (518) 457-5434
TDD: (800) 634-2110 (out of state) or (518) 485-5082 (foreign locations)

North Carolina

North Carolina Department of Revenue
www.dornc.com
Physical address:
501 N. Wilmington St.
Raleigh, NC 27604
Mailing address:
Refund Due:
North Carolina Department of Revenue
P.O. Box R
Raleigh, NC 27634-0001
North Carolina Department of Revenue
P.O. Box 25000
Raleigh, NC 27640-0640
General information:
Central Collection Unity
501 N. Wilmington St.
Raleigh, NC 27604

Collection Division Offices

Asheville Collection Division Office
North Carolina Department of Revenue
2800 Heart Dr.
Asheville, NC 28806
Phone: (828) 667-0597
Fax: (828) 667-0354

Charlotte Collection Division Office
North Carolina Department of Revenue
5111 Nations Crossing Rd., Bldg. 8, Suite 100
Charlotte, NC 28217
Phone: (704) 519-3000
Fax: (704) 586-1432

Durham Collection Division Office
North Carolina Department of Revenue
3518 Westgate Dr., Suite 100
Durham, NC 27707
Phone: (919) 627-6900
Fax: (919) 560-3386

Elizabeth City Collection Division Office
North Carolina Department of Revenue
401 South Griffin St., Suite 300
Elizabeth City, NC 27906
Mailing address:
NC Department of Revenue
P.O. Box 1130
Elizabeth City, NC 27906-1130

Fayetteville Collection Division Office
North CarolinaNorth Carolina225 Green St., Suite 800
Fayetteville, NC 28301
Phone: (910) 486-1212
Fax: (910) 486-1030

Greensboro Collection Division Office
North Carolina Department of Revenue
5 Centerview Dr., Suite 100
Lenoir Building, Kroger Center
Greensboro, NC 27407
Phone: (336) 315-7001
Fax: (336) 315-7010

Greenville Collection Division Office
North Carolina Department of Revenue
2995 Radio Station Rd.
Greenville, NC 27834

Phone: (252) 830-8534
Fax: (252) 830-3168

Hickory Collection Division Office
North Carolina Department of Revenue
112 2nd St., Place SE
Hickory, NC 28602
Mailing address:
NC Department of Revenue
P.O. Box 2110
Hickory, NC 28603-2110
Phone: (828) 327-7474
Fax: (828) 327-7615

Raleigh Collection Division Office
North Carolina Department of Revenue
4701 Atlantic Ave., Suite 118
Raleigh, NC 27604
Mailing address:
NC Department of Revenue
P.O. Box 58787
Raleigh, NC 27658-8787
Phone: (919) 707-0800
Fax: (919) 850-2953

Rocky Mount Collection Division Office
North Carolina Department of Revenue
110 Fountain Park Dr., Suite F-1
Battleboro, NC 27809
Phone: (252) 467-9200
Fax: (252) 467-0823

Wilmington Collection Division Office
North Carolina Department of Revenue
3340 Jaeckle Dr., Suite 202
Wilmington, NC 28403
Phone: (910) 254-5000
Fax: (910) 251-5823

Winston Salem Collection Division Office
North Carolina Department of Revenue
8025 Northpoint Blvd., Suite 250
Winston Salem, NC 27106
Phone: (336) 896-7026
Fax: (336) 896-7030

General information: (877) 252-3052
Department of Revenue: (877) 252-3252

North Dakota

Office of State Tax Commissioner, Bismark, North Dakota
www.nd.gov/tax
Physical address:
Office of State Tax Commissioner
600 E. Boulevard Ave., Dept. 127
Bismarck, ND 58505-0599

Remote Offices

Office of State Tax Commissioner
P.O. Box 766
Dickinson, ND 58602-0766

Office of State Tax Commissioner
3217 Fiechtner Dr. South
Fargo, ND 58103-8735

Office of State Tax Commissioner
P.O. Box 14435
Grand Forks, ND 58208-4435

Office of State Tax Commissioner
1600 2nd Ave., SW, Suite 11
Minot, ND 58701-3459

Office of State Tax Commissioner
P.O. Box 1701
Williston, ND 58802-1701

Phone: (701) 328-7088 or toll-free: (877) 328-7088
TDD: (800) 366-6888

State Departments of Revenue Contact Information 189

Fax: (701) 328-3700
Individual Income Tax: (701) 328-1247
Accounts Receivable: (701) 328-1244

Ohio

Ohio Department of Taxation
tax.ohio.gov
Tax Commissioners Office:
30 E. Broad St., 22nd Floor
Columbus, OH 43215
Mailing address:
Ohio Department of Taxation
P.O. Box 530
Columbus, OH 43216-0530

Compliance Division
4485 Northland Ridge Blvd.
Columbus, OH 43229

Tax Commissioner's Office
Phone: (614) 446-2166
Fax: (614) 466-6401
General: (614) 387-1801
Fax: (614) 387-1849
Individual Taxpayer Assistance: (800) 282-1780
Business Taxpayer Assistance: (888) 405-4039
Compliance Division: (614) 387-1701
Fax: (614) 387-1847
Income Tax Refund Hotline: (800) 282-1784
TDD: (800) 750-0750

Oklahoma

Oklahoma Tax Commission
www.tax.ok.gov
Mailing addresses:
Individual Income Tax Form 511
Oklahoma Tax Commission

P.O. Box 26800
Oklahoma City, OK 73126-0800
Individual Income Tax 2D Form 511
Oklahoma Tax Commission
P.O. Box 269045
Oklahoma City, OK 73126-9045
Toll-free (in-state): (800) 522-8165
Taxpayer Assistance: (405) 521-3160
Assessment Letters (Income Tax): (405) 522-5737
Collection Information: (405) 521-3281

Oregon

Oregon Department of Revenue
www.oregon.gov/DOR
Physical address:
Oregon Department of Revenue
955 Center St. NE
Salem, OR 97301-2555

District Offices

Bend
951 SW Simpson Ave., Suite 100
Bend, OR 97702-3118
Phone: (541) 388-6139

Coos Bay
1155 S. 5th St., Suite A
Coos Bay, OR 97420
Phone: (541) 266-0217

Eugene
1600 Valley River Dr., Suite 310
Eugene, OR 97401-2160
Phone: (541) 686-7935

Gresham
1550 NW Eastman Pkwy., Suite 220
Gresham, OR 97030-3832
Phone: (503) 674-6272

Medford
3613 Aviation Way, Suite 102
Medford, OR 97504-6010
Phone: (541) 858-6500

Newport
119 4th St., NE #4
Newport, OR 97365
Phone: (541) 265-5139

Pendleton
700 SE Emigrant, Suite 310
Pendleton, OR 97801
Phone: (541) 278-6851

Portland
800 NE Oregon St., Suite 505
Portland, OR 97232-2156
Phone: (971) 673-0700

General: (503) 378-4988 or (800) 356-4222
TTY: (800) 886-7204
Personal Income Tax Help: (503) 378-4988
Business/Corporate Tax Help: (503) 378-4988

Pennsylvania

Pennsylvania Department of Revenue
www.revenue.state.pa.us

Central Area Offices

PA Department of Revenue
Scranton District Office
Samters Bldg., Room 201
101 Penn Ave.
Scranton, PA 18563-1970

Delinquent Collections Coordinator
Strawberry Square, 10th Floor
Harrisburg, PA 17128-1210

Delinquent Collections Coordinator
Phone: (717) 772-6991
Fax: (717) 772-5118

Personal Income Tax Delinquency
Phone: (717) 783-3000

Rhode Island

State of Rhode Island Division of Taxation – Department of Revenue
www.tax.state.ri.us
Physical address:
Rhode Island Division of Taxation
One Capitol Hill
Providence, RI 02908
Collections: (401) 574-8941
Electronic Filings of Personal Income Tax: (401) 574-8829
Personal Income Tax – TPA: (401) 574-8829

South Carolina

South Carolina Department of Revenue
www.sctax.org
Mailing address:
Individual Income Return:
SC1040 or SC1040NR-Refunds or No Tax Due

Long Form Processing Center
P.O. Box 101100
Columbia, SC 29211-0100

All Balance Dues
Taxable Processing Center
P.O. Box 101105
Columbia, SC 29211-0105

Taxpayer Service Centers

Charleston Service Center
1 S. Park Cir., Suite 100

State Departments of Revenue Contact Information

Charleston, 29407
Phone: (843) 852-3600
Fax: (843) 556-1780

Columbia Main Office
301 Gervais St.
P.O. Box 125
Columbia, SC 29214
Phone: (803) 898-5000
Fax: (803) 898-5822

Florence Service Center
1452 West Evans St.
P.O. Box 5418
Florence, SC 29502
Phone: (843) 661-4850
Fax: (843) 662-4876

Greenville Service Center
211 Century Dr., Suite 210-B
Greenville, SC 29607
Phone: (864) 241-1200
Fax: (864) 232-5008

Myrtle Beach Service Center
1330 Howard Pkwy
P.O. Box 30427
Myrtle Beach, SC 29588
Phone: (843) 839-2960
Fax: (843) 839-2664

Rock Hill Service Center
Business and Technology Center
454 S. Anderson Rd., Suite 202
P.O. Box 12099
Rock Hill, SC 29731
Phone: (803) 324-7641
Fax: (803) 324-8289

Income Tax Refunds: (803) 898-5300
Income Tax Assistance: (803) 898-5709
Compliance and Recovery: (803) 896-1100

TTY: (800) 676-3777 (outside SC) or 711 (in SC)
Taxpayer Advocate: (803) 898-5444
VITA: (803) 898-5405

South Dakota

South Dakota Department of Revenue and Regulation
www.state.sd.us/drr2
Business Tax Division:
445 E. Capitol Ave.
Pierre, SC 57501
Phone: (800) 829-9188 or (605) 773-3311
Fax: (605) 773-6729
E-mail: bustax@state.sd.us

Special Taxes Division:
445 E. Capitol Ave.
Pierre, SC 57501
Phone: (605) 773-3311
Fax: (605) 773-6729

Tennessee

Tennessee Department of Revenue
www.tn.gov/revenue
Mail tax payments to:
Tennessee Department of Revenue
Andrew Jackson Bldg.
500 Deaderick St.
Nashville, TN 37242

Tax Information
Statewide toll-free: (800) 342-1003
Nashville-area and out-of-state: (615) 253-0600
Tax Practitioner Hotline:
Statewide toll-free: (800) 397-8395
Nashville-area and out-of-state: (615) 253-0700
Fax: (615) 253-3580

State Departments of Revenue Contact Information

Streamlined Sales Tax Information
Statewide toll-free: (877) 250-2299
Nashville-area and out-of-state: (615) 253-0752
E-mail: Streamlined.Salestax.QandA@tn.gov

Electronic Commerce Hot Line
Statewide toll-free: (866) 368-6374
Nashville-area and out-of-state: (615) 253-0704
Local Government Hot Line: (866) 562-2549
Tax Fraud Hot Line: (800) FRAUDTX or (800) 372-8389
Penalty Waivers: (615) 532-6464
Refunds: (615) 741-0443
Voluntary Disclosure: (615) 741-8319
Franchise and Excise Tax Reinstatements and Dissolutions: (615) 741-8999

Individual Income Tax
Audit Staff: (615) 532-6439
Statewide toll-free: (800) 342-1003
Nashville-area and out-of-state: (615) 253-0600
Inheritance, Estate, and Gift Taxes:
Audit Staff: (615) 532-6438

Liquor-by-the-Drink Tax Technical Information
Bonds: (615) 532-4552
Statewide toll-free: (800) 342-1003
Nashville-area and out-of-state: (615) 253-0600

Texas

Texas Comptroller's Office
www.window.state.tx.us/taxes

Field Offices

Abilene
Taxpayer Services and Collections
209 S. Danville Dr., Suite C-202
Abilene, TX 79605-1464
Phone: (325) 695-4323
Audit Office

209 S. Danville Dr., Suite C-222
Abilene, TX 79605-1464
Phone: (325) 695-4323

Amarillo
Field Office
Taxpayer Services and Collections
Park West Office Centre, Bldg. A
7120 W. Interstate 40, Suite 220
Amarillo, TX 79106-2519
Phone: (806) 358-0148
Audit Office
Park W. Office Centre, Bldg. A
7120 W. Interstate 40, Suite 240
Amarillo, TX 79106-2516
Phone: (806) 358-0148

Austin
Field Office
Taxpayer Services and Collections
Central Services Bldg.
1711 San Jacinto Blvd., Suite 180
Austin, TX 78701-1416
Phone: (512) 463-4865
Audit Office
Central Services Building
1711 San Jacinto Blvd., 3rd Floor
Austin, TX 78701-1416
Phone: (512) 305-9800

Beaumont
Field Office
Taxpayer Services and Collections
6440 Concord Rd.
Beaumont, TX 77708-4315
Phone: (409) 899-4650
Audit Office
6442 Concord Rd.
Beaumont, TX 77708-4315
Phone: (409) 899-4650

State Departments of Revenue Contact Information

Brownsville
Field Office
Taxpayer Services and Collections
1900 N. Expressway, Suite C-1
Brownsville, TX 78521-1563
Phone: (956) 542-8426

Bryan
Field Office
Taxpayer Services and Collections
1713 Broadmoor Dr., Suite 300
Bryan, TX 77802-5220
Phone: (979) 776-5200

Corpus Christi
Field Office
Taxpayer Services and Collections
400 Mann St., Suite 600
Corpus Christi, TX 78401-2047
Phone: (361) 882-1234
Audit Office
400 Mann St., Suite 608
Corpus Christi, Texas 78401-2047
Phone: (361) 882-1234

Dallas
Field Office – Dallas Northeast
Taxpayer Services and Collections
9221 LBJ Freeway, Suite 100
Dallas, Texas 75243-3429
Phone: (972) 792-5800
Field Office – Dallas Southwest
Taxpayer Services and Collections
7222 S. Westmoreland Road, Suite 100
Dallas, TX 75237-2983
Phone: (972) 709-4357
Audit Office – Dallas East
9221 LBJ Freeway, Suite 200
Dallas, TX 75243-3455
Phone: (972) 792-5800

Audit Office – Dallas West
2655 Villa Creek Dr., Suite 270
Dallas, TX 75234-7316
Phone: (972) 888-5300

Denton
Field Office
Taxpayer Services and Collections
400 S. Carroll Blvd., Suite 1000
Denton,TX 76201-5929
Phone: (940) 891-4790

El Paso
Field Office
Taxpayer Services and Collections
401 E. Franklin Ave., Suite 160
El Paso, TX 79901
Phone: (915) 533-0506
Audit Office
401 E. Franklin Ave., Suite 170
El Paso, TX 79901
Phone: (915) 533-0506

Fort Worth
Field Office
Taxpayer Services and Collections
4040 Fossil Creek Blvd., Suite 100
Fort Worth, TX 76137-2747
Phone: (817) 847-6201
Audit Office
Crosslands Plaza
6320 Southwest Blvd., Suite 201
Fort Worth, TX 76109
Phone: (817) 377-8855

Houston
Field Office – Houston Northwest
Taxpayer Services and Collections
1919 North Loop West, Suite 510
Houston, TX 77008-1354

State Departments of Revenue Contact Information

Phone: (713) 426-8200
Field Office – Houston Southwest
Taxpayer Services and Collections
7011 Harwin Dr., Suite 186
Houston, TX 77036-2151
Phone: (713) 783-1665
Audit Office – Houston North
1919 North Loop West, Suite 311
Houston, TX 77008-1394
Phone: (713) 426-8200
Audit Office – Houston South
2656 South Loop West, Suite 400
Houston, TX 77054-2600
Phone: (713) 314-5700
Audit Office – Houston West
1260 Pin Oak Rd., Suite 210
Katy, TX 77494-5600
Phone: (281) 371-5500

Laredo
Field Office
Taxpayer Services and Collections
1202 E. Del Mar Blvd., Suite 1
Laredo, TX 78041-2400
Phone: (956) 722-2859
Lubbock
Field Office
Taxpayer Services and Collections
6202 Iola Ave., Suite 900-B
Lubbock, TX 79424-2733
Phone: (806) 783-0316
Audit Office
6202 Iola Ave., Suite 900-B
Lubbock, TX 79424-2733
Phone: (806) 783-0316

Lufkin
Field Office
Taxpayer Services and Collections

306 Harmony Hill Dr., Suite A
Lufkin, TX 75901-5759
Phone: (936) 634-2621

McAllen
Field Office
Taxpayer Services and Collections
3231 N. McColl Rd.
McAllen, TX 78501-5538
Phone: (956) 687-9227
Audit Office
3231 N. McColl Rd.
McAllen, TX 78501-5538
Phone: (956) 687-9227

Odessa
Field Office
Taxpayer Services and Collections
4682 E. University Blvd., Suite 200
Odessa, TX 79762-8104
Phone: (432) 550-3027
Audit Office
4682 E. University Blvd., Suite 200
Odessa, TX 79762-8104
Phone: (432) 550-3027

San Angelo
Field Office
Taxpayer Services and Collections
3127 Executive Dr.
San Angelo, TX 76904-6801
Phone: (325) 942-8364

San Antonio
Field Office – San Antonio Northeast
Taxpayer Services and Collections
3300 Nacogdoches Rd., Suite 105
San Antonio, TX 78217-3373
Phone: (210) 646-0399
Field Office – San Antonio Northwest

Taxpayer Services and Collections
9514 Console Dr., Suite 102
San Antonio, TX 78229-2042
Phone: (210) 616-0067
Field Office – San Antonio Southwest
Taxpayer Services and Collections
123 Southwest Military Dr.
San Antonio, TX 78221-1650
Phone: (210) 924-6434
Audit Office
6875 Bandera Road
San Antonio, TX 78238-1359
Phone: (210) 257-4600

Sherman
Field Office
Taxpayer Services and Collections
One Grand Centre Bldg.
1800 Teague Dr., Suite 110
Sherman, TX 75090-2672
Phone: (903) 893-0692

Tyler
Field Office
Taxpayer Services and Collections
3800 Paluxy Dr., Suite 300
Tyler, TX 75703-1661
Phone: (903) 534-0333
Audit Office
3800 Paluxy Dr., Suite 300
Tyler, TX 75703-1661
Phone: (903) 534-0333

Victoria
Field Office
Taxpayer Services and Collections
2208 Leary Lane, Suite 200
Victoria, TX 77904
Phone: (361) 575-2874

Waco
Field Office
Taxpayer Services and Collections
801 Austin Ave., Suite 810
Waco, TX 76701-1937
Phone: (254) 752-3147
Audit Office
801 Austin Ave., Suite 940
Waco, TX 76701-1941
Phone: (254) 752-3147

Wichita Falls
Field Office
Taxpayer Services and Collections
925 Lamar St., Suite 1900
Wichita Falls, TX 76301-3414
Phone: (940) 761-4141

Chicago, Illinois
Audit Office
2809 Butterfield Road, Suite 340
Oak Brook, Illinois 60523-1196
Phone: (630) 574-5120

Los Angeles, California
Audit Office
17777 Center Court Drive North, Suite 700
Cerritos, California 90703
Phone: (562) 402-2000
New York, New York
Audit Office
215 Lexington Ave., 19th Floor
New York, New York 10016
Phone: (646) 742-1155

Tulsa, Oklahoma
Audit Office
Towne Centre, Bldg. C
10830 E. 45th St., Suite 201
Tulsa, Oklahoma 74146-3809
Phone: (918) 622-4311

State Departments of Revenue Contact Information

Utah

Utah State Tax Commission
http://tax.utah.gov
Mailing address:
Utah State Tax Commission
210 N. 1950 West
Salt Lake City, UT 84134

Returns with Refunds
Utah State Tax Commission
210 N. 1950 West
Salt Lake City, UT 84134-0260
Payments, Returns with Payments, and all Non-Refund Returns:
Utah State Tax Commission
210 N. 1950 West
Salt Lake City, UT 84134-0266

Other Locations

Ogden Tax Commission
2540 Washington Blvd., 7th Floor
Ogden, UT 84401
Phone: (801) 626-3460
Fax: (801) 626-3446

Provo Tax Commission
150 East Center, #1300
Provo, UT 84606
Phone: (801) 374-7070
Fax: (801) 374-7089

Washington County Tax Commission
100 S. 5300 West
Hurricane, UT 84737
Phone: (435) 251-9520
Fax: (435) 251-9529

General phone number: (801) 297-2200 or (800) 662-4335
TPA: (801) 297-7562
E-mail: taxpayeradvocate@utah.gov
Collections Division: (435) 251-9520

Vermont

Vermont Department of Taxes
www.state.vt.us/tax
Mailing address:
Income Tax Payments, Including Estimated Voucher
Vermont Department of Taxes
P.O. Box 1779
Montpelier, VT 05601-1779

Income Tax Refund No Balance Due or No Payment
Vermont Department of Taxes
P.O. Box 1881
Montpelier, VT 05601-1881

General Correspondence
Vermont Department of Taxes
133 State St.
Montpelier, VT 05633-1401

Administration
Commissioner, Policy Analysts:
Phone: (802) 828-2505
Fax: (802) 828-2701
Collections:
Phone: (802) 828-2518
Fax: (802) 828-5282
Individual Income Tax:
Phone: (866) 828-2865 (toll-free in VT) or (802) 828-2865 (local and out-of-state)
Fax: (802) 828-2720

Virginia

Virginia Department of Taxation
www.tax.virginia.gov
Mailing address:
Virginia Department of Taxation
Office of Customer Services
P.O. Box 1115

State Departments of Revenue Contact Information

Richmond, VA 23218-1115
Walk-in Customer Assistance
3610 W. Broad
Richmond, VA 23230
Customer Service: (804) 367-8031
Fax: (804) 254-6113
Collections: (804) 367-8045
Fax: (804) 254-6112

Washington

Department of Revenue
www.dor.wa.gov
Washington State Department of Revenue
Taxpayer Account Administration
P.O. Box 47476
Olympia, WA 98504-7476
Phone: (800) 647-7706

West Virginia

West Virginia State Tax Department
www.wvtax.gov
Mailing address:
West Virginia State Tax Department
Taxpayer Services Division
P.O. Box 3784
Charleston, WV 25337-3784
Compliance Division

Internal Collections Unit
P.O. Box 229
Charleston, WV 25321

Taxpayer Services

Beckley
407 Neville St., Suite 109
Beckley, WV 25801
Phone: (304) 256-6764

Charleston
1206 Quarrier St.
Charleston, WV 25301
Phone: (304) 558-3333 or (800) 982-8297

Huntington
2699 Park Ave., Suite 230
Huntington, WV 25704
Phone: (304) 528-5568

Martinsburg
397 Mid Atlantic Pkwy., Suite 2
Martinsburg, WV 25401
Phone: (304) 267-0022

Clarksburg
Huntington Bank Bldg., Suite 201
230 W. Pike St.
Clarksburg, WV 26301
Phone: (304) 627-2109

Parkersburg
400 5th St
Parkersburg, WV 26101
Phone: (304) 420-4570

Wheeling
40 14th St.
Wheeling, WV 26003
Phone: (304) 238-1152

General Assistance: (304) 558-3333 or (800) 982-8297
TDD Service: (800) 282-9833 or (800) TAXTDD
Compliance Department: (304) 558-8753
E-mail: compintcol@tax.state.wv.us

Wisconsin

Wisconsin Department of Revenue
www.revenue.wi.gov
Mailing address:
Wisconsin Department of Revenue

Individual Income Tax Assistance
P.O. Box 8906
Madison, WI 53708-8906

Office Locations

Madison Headquarters
2135 Rimrock Rd.
Madison, WI 53713
Phone: (608) 266-2772
Fax: (608) 267-0834

Appleton
265 W. Northland Ave.
Appleton, WI 54911-2016
Phone: (920) 832-2727
Fax: (920) 832-2909

Eau Claire
718 W. Clairemont Ave.
Eau Claire, WI 54701-4558
Phone: (715) 836-2811
Fax: (715) 836-6691

Milwaukee
819 N. Sixth St., Room 408
Milwaukee, WI 53203-1606
Phone: (414) 227-4000
Fax: (414) 227-4405

Individual Taxpayers: (608) 266-2772
Business: Taxpayers: (608) 266-2776
Fax: (608) 267-0834
Delinquent Taxes: (608) 266-7879
Individual Income: (608) 266-2486

Wyoming

Wyoming Department of Revenue
http://revenue.state.wy.us
Herschler Bldg., 2nd Floor W.

Cheyenne, WY 82002-0110
Phone: (307) 777-7961
E-mail: DirectorOfRevenue@wy.gov

About JK Harris

JK Harris is an author, entrepreneur, and founder and CEO of JK Harris & Company, the nation's largest tax representation firm. JK Harris & Company also provides business services such as accounting, bookkeeping, tax preparation, and other consulting services to small businesses nationwide.

The son of a schoolteacher and a federal government employee, JK (John) Harris grew up on a dairy farm in rural South Carolina, which introduced him to a wide range of important business fundamentals at an early age. He attended Carlisle Military School in Bamberg, South Carolina, where he played basketball and baseball, developed his leadership skills, and graduated as salutatorian of his class. Continuing his education, he worked full time while attending the University of South Carolina, graduating cum laude with a degree in history and political science in 1976. He went on to earn his master's in accounting in 1977 and received his Certified Public Accountant certificate the following year.

His first post-college job was as a staff accountant at Haskins & Sells, CPAs (now Deloitte Touche Tohmatsu) in Charlotte, North Carolina. Over the years, he has been the founder, owner, or co-owner of businesses in a range of industries, including automotive and construction, as well as business, consumer, and professional services.

Harris opened his accounting practice in 1996 to share his business expertise with other entrepreneurs in the Charleston area. When a new accounting client came to him owing the IRS $90,000, Harris was able to settle it for $42,000. In the process, he realized that there was a significant lack of qualified assistance for taxpayers who were in debt to the IRS. He decided that JK Harris & Company would focus on those services and in 1997 decided to grow his two-person accounting practice into the nation's largest tax representation firm. Today, with 325 offices in 43 states and annual sales of more than $50 million, JK Harris & Company continues to lead the tax representation industry, and Harris continues to serve as president and CEO of the firm.

Crediting much of his success to lessons learned from other entrepreneurs as well as his own experience, Harris has made it his mission to share his knowledge and expertise with business owners and managers across the country and throughout the world through his books and speeches. In 2009, he wrote his first book, F*lashpoint: Seven Core Strategies for Rapid-Fire Business Growt*h. That was followed by *Sales Flashpoint: 15 Strategies for Rapid-Fire Sales Growth*, and he is currently working on the next book in the Flashpoints series, along with a series of teleseminars and e-books.

Invite JK Harris to Speak at Your Event

JK (John) Harris is an engaging speaker with a valuable message about how you can take your business to the Flashpoint of growth and profitability. Harris' dynamic and provocative presentations are designed to entertain, inform, and motivate. His audiences leave energized, enthused, and ready to take action.

JK Harris accepts a limited number of speaking engagements each year. To book him for your event, visit www.theflashpoints.com today.

JK Harris & Company

For a no-charge, no-obligation personal consultation about your tax issues, contact JK Harris & Company today.

Give us a call at
(800) 800-3022
or visit
www.jkharris.com

JK Harris & Company
Corporate Headquarters
208-A St. James Ave.
Goose Creek, SC 29445

flashpoints

Are you a business owner or manager?

If so, please accept these two free gifts from JK Harris

The first is JK Harris' exciting e-book, *The Mindset of High Achievers*. Find out how high achievers think, how their mindset affects what they are able to accomplish, and how you can use the same techniques and strategies they do to achieve more with far less effort than you ever dreamed possible.

The second is a complimentary subscription to *Flashpoints* newsletter. Get JK Harris' wisdom and business acumen delivered via e-mail. Each month, *Flashpoints* will bring you timely articles and resources to help you deal with issues related to starting and managing a fast-growing, profitable company—all absolutely free.

Help take your company to the Flashpoint by accepting these two free gifts from JK Harris. Visit www.theflashpoints.com to claim your gifts today.